STOCK INVESTING 101
*A Beginner's Guide to Building
Wealth with Smart Investing*

Usiere Uko

Copyright © 2023 Usiere Uko

All Rrghts reserved.

No part of this publication may be reproduced, distributed, or transmitted in any form or by any means, including photocopying, recording, or other electronic or mechanical methods, without the prior written permission of the publisher, except in the case of brief quotations embodied in critical reviews and certain other noncommercial uses permitted by copyright law.
This publication is designed to provide accurate and authoritative information in regard to the subject matter covered. It is sold with the understanding that the publisher is not engaged in rendering legal, accounting, or other professional services. If legal advice or other expert assistance is required, the services of a competent professional should be sought.
The author and publisher shall not be liable for any loss of profit or any other commercial damages, including but not limited to special, incidental, consequential, or other damages.

ISBN-13: 979-8-376-26966-4

FIRST EDITION

...To new beginnings

CONTENTS

Title Page
Copyright
Dedication
INTRODUCTION
1: INTRODUCTION TO STOCK MARKET INVESTING — 1
2: PRIMARY AND SECONDARY MARKET — 5
3: UNDERSTANDING THE STOCK MARKET — 9
4: TYPES OF INDIVIDUAL STOCK INVESTORS — 13
5: TYPES OF STOCKS AND STOCK MARKET INDICES — 15
6: WHY INVEST IN STOCKS? — 18
7: HOW SAFE ARE STOCKS? — 21
8: FUNDAMENTAL STOCK INVESTING — 24
9: TECHNICAL STOCK INVESTING — 28
10: HOW TO READ STOCK CHARTS — 32
11: EVALUATING COMPANIES AND STOCKS — 36
12: RISK MANAGEMENT STRATEGIES — 39
13: DEVELOPING A STOCK INVESTING PLAN — 42
14: DIFFERENT WAYS TO INVEST IN THE STOCK MARKET — 44
15: ONLINE AND OFFLINE STOCK TRADING — 47
16: CHOOSING A BROKERAGE — 50
17: OPENING AND MANAGING A BROKERAGE ACCOUNT — 53

18: PLACING TRADES AND EXECUTING ORDERS	55
19: MARKET ORDERS, LIMIT ORDERS, AND STOP ORDERS	57
20: STRATEGIES FOR STOCK MARKET INVESTING	59
21: LONG-TERM AND SHORT-TERM INVESTING	62
22: STOCK MARKET INDEX FUNDS AND ETFs	65
23: UNDERSTANDING FINANCIAL STATEMENTS	68
24: BASICS OF INCOME INVESTING	71
25: PRINCIPLE OF VALUE INVESTING	75
26: THE CONTRARIAN INVESTOR	78
27: INVESTING IN IPOS	83
28: INVESTING WITH MUTUAL FUNDS	86
29: MARGIN TRADING	89
30: YOUR EXIT STRATEGY	92
31: ONLINE STOCK TRADING	95
32: THE ROLE OF NEWS AND MEDIA IN THE STOCK MARKET	98
33: TAX IMPLICATIONS OF STOCK MARKET INVESTING	100
34: THE PSYCHOLOGY OF TRADING THE STOCK MARKET	102
35: COMMON MISTAKES TO AVOID	104
36: STRATEGIES FOR SUCCESS IN STOCK MARKET INVESTING	107
37: BUILDING A STOCK PORTFOLIO	109
38: CONCLUSION AND NEXT STEPS	112
About The Author	115
Books In This Series	117
Books By This Author	119

INTRODUCTION
OWNING A STAKE IN EXISTING COMPANIES

I bought my first stock in 1999. Prior to that time, buying shares in companies was an abstract term, something only millionaires who sit on company boards could afford to do. The only source of income I was aware of back then was your salary at the end of each month or from your own business.

Running a business was outside my reality. Everyone close to me aspired to go to a good school, earn a good degree in order to get a good job.

Nobody told me, neither was I aware of anyone who owned shares in a company, until a colleague who usually travelled abroad for vacation every summer opened my eyes to investing in the stock market. At some point she mentioned that she purchased her flight ticket from the proceeds of dividend from one of her stocks. She was shocked to learn I had no single share to my name. A few days later, she took me to her stockbroker to open account open a stock broking account to start buying and selling stocks.

That was my introduction to the world of stocks. I remember thinking if I had known about stocks earlier, I would have bought stocks while in the university rather than save up to furnish my flat after graduation. The stuff I bought then depreciated and was eventually given away while stocks appreciated during the same period, in price, dividends paid and bonuses given. The shares would have made me richer rather than the stuff that I bought which eventually ended up in the trash.

If you have been investing in the money market, the stock market is a different ball game. The risk is higher so is the reward. Your capital (net worth) gets to grow while you earn income, which is if you know what you are doing.

Standard wisdom and commonsense applies; invest in knowing what you are doing first before you spend your money. If you don't know what you are doing, your lessons become very expensive. This means you lose control over how much you pay as tuition, leaving you at the mercy of the market.

Investing in the stock market requires a different mindset from that required for investing in the money market. Your return on investment is not guaranteed, neither is your return of investment. You have to carry out your due diligence to determine which company to invest in or stock to buy. You have to step out of your comfort zone and get comfortable gaining knowledge outside your area of core competence.

Investing in the stock market can be a very rewarding experience. Your wealth grows with the companies you wisely invested in, especially young companies that grow bigger over time.

Many have become millionaires through investing in stocks. Some have made it to the billionaire list through investing in stocks. One of the richest men in the world, Warren Buffet aka the Sage of Omaha became rich through investing in stocks.

Investing in stocks is not a rocket science. It is something you can learn if you make up your mind to. Picking up this book is an indication that you are willing to commence your journey. If you make up your mind to pay the price necessary, you will achieve your goal and beyond.

1: INTRODUCTION TO STOCK MARKET INVESTING

The stock market is a platform where publicly traded companies list their shares of ownership for investors to buy and sell. The stock market provides a way for companies to raise capital by issuing shares of stock to the public, and for investors to potentially earn a return on their investment by buying and selling these shares.

In this chapter, we will provide an overview of stock market investing and its importance for individuals who want to invest in the market.

UNDERSTANDING THE STOCK MARKET

The stock market is a complex system of exchanges, where investors can buy and sell securities such as stocks, bonds, and options. The two main stock exchanges in the United States are the New York Stock Exchange (NYSE) and the Nasdaq Stock Market.

The stock market is a reflection of the economy and can be influenced by a variety of factors, including government policies, company performance, and global events.

BENEFITS OF STOCK MARKET INVESTING

Stock market investing offers the potential for higher returns compared to other investment options such as savings accounts or bonds.

30 Year Dow Jones Industrial Average (DJIA). Image: macrotrends.net

Over the long-term, investing in the stock market has historically provided average annual returns of around 7-10%.

This can help individuals grow their wealth and achieve financial goals such as retirement or buying a home.

TYPES OF INVESTORS

Individual investors, institutional investors, and day traders are the three main types of investors in the stock market.

Individual investors are everyday people who invest their own money in the market.

Institutional investors are large organizations such as pension funds, mutual funds, or hedge funds.

Day traders are individuals who buy and sell securities within the same trading day to take advantage of short-term price movements.

TYPES OF SECURITIES

There are many types of securities that can be traded on the stock market, including stocks, bonds, options, and mutual funds.

Stocks represent ownership in a company and give investors the right to vote on company matters and receive dividends.

Bonds are debt securities that represent a loan made to a company or government entity.

Options are contracts that give the holder the right, but not the obligation, to buy or sell an underlying asset at a predetermined price.

Mutual funds are investment vehicles that pool money from many investors to purchase a diversified portfolio of stocks or bonds.

RISKS OF STOCK MARKET INVESTING

While stock market investing offers the potential for higher returns, it also comes with risks. The stock market can be volatile, and the value of stocks can fluctuate based on a variety of factors.

Investors can also lose money if they make poor investment decisions or do not manage their portfolio properly. It is important to have a solid understanding of the market and develop a long-term investment strategy to help mitigate these risks.

APPROACHES TO STOCK MARKET INVESTING

There are several approaches to stock market investing, including fundamental analysis, technical analysis, and a combination of both.

Fundamental analysis involves analyzing a company's financial statements and business operations to determine its value and growth potential.

Technical analysis involves analyzing stock charts and price movements to identify patterns and predict future market trends.

A combination of both approaches can be used to create a well-rounded investment strategy.

Stock market investing is an important tool for individuals who want to grow their wealth over time. Understanding the basics of the stock market, the types of securities that can be traded, and the risks involved, and the different approaches to investing can help individuals make informed investment decisions. In the next chapters, we will dive deeper into these topics.

2: PRIMARY AND SECONDARY MARKET

The stock market is typically divided into two main categories: primary and secondary markets.

PRIMARY MARKET

The primary stock market, also known as the new issue market, is a financial market where companies issue and sell their stocks to the public for the first time, usually through an initial public offering (IPO). However, companies can also issue stocks in the primary market through private placements and equity placements.

An initial public offering (IPO) is the process by which a company goes public by offering its shares to the public for the first time. In an IPO, the company hires an investment bank, or underwriter, to help it determine the offering price and the number of shares to be sold. The underwriter then markets the shares to potential investors and helps to facilitate the sale of the securities.

During the IPO, the company typically sells a portion of its shares to the public, while retaining some of the shares for its existing shareholders. The shares are sold on a stock exchange, such as the New York Stock Exchange (NYSE) or NASDAQ, and the company's shares begin trading publicly.

An IPO can be an important event for a company, as it provides the company with access to capital to finance growth and expansion plans. It can also increase the company's visibility and credibility in the market.

Private placements are a way for companies to raise capital by selling shares to a select group of investors, such as institutional investors or high net worth individuals, without going through the public IPO process.

Private placements are typically less expensive and less time-consuming than an IPO, and they allow companies to raise capital without having to comply with as many regulatory requirements.

Equity placements are another type of primary market transaction where companies issue shares to a small group of investors, but unlike private placements, they are usually done in conjunction with an IPO. In an equity placement, the company sells shares to institutional investors or other large investors before the IPO takes place.

The equity placement helps to ensure that the IPO will be successful, as the large investors commit to buying shares in the IPO, providing the company with a guaranteed source of demand.

The primary market provides an avenue for companies to raise capital to fund their operations or expansion plans. It provides investors with an opportunity to invest in new and promising companies or other issuers.

However, investing in the primary market can be risky, and it is important for investors to carefully evaluate the financial health and prospects of the issuer before investing in its securities.

SECONDARY MARKET

The secondary market is where previously issued securities are bought and sold between investors without the involvement of the issuing company. The secondary market provides liquidity to investors who want to buy or sell their securities, allowing them to easily enter or exit their positions.

The price at which a stock is bought or sold is determined by the supply and demand for the stock. If more investors are interested in buying a stock than selling it, the price of the stock will generally rise. Conversely, if more investors are interested in selling a stock than buying it, the price of the stock will generally fall.

Issuers can monitor the trading activity of their stocks on the secondary market and use this information to gauge investor sentiment and adjust their financial strategies accordingly.

Additionally, companies can issue new stocks or buy back existing stocks in the secondary market through intermediaries such as investment banks or broker-dealers. However, such transactions are typically subject to regulatory requirements and approval processes.

***

There are different stock exchanges around the world, with the most famous ones being the New York Stock Exchange (NYSE) and the NASDAQ in the United States. There is the London Stock Exchange in the UK, Nigerian Stock Exchange in Nigeria, etc.

The value of a stock is determined by supply and demand, with the price of a stock fluctuating based on market conditions and investors' perceptions of the company's future performance.

Image: freerangestock.com

The stock market typically exhibits three primary trends: upward, downward, or sideways. A rising trend is referred to as a "bull market" or "bullish," while a falling trend is known as a "bear market" or "bearish." When prices are relatively stable and move sideways, the market is said to be consolidating.

3: UNDERSTANDING THE STOCK MARKET

To become a successful stock market investor, it is essential to have a good understanding of how the market works.

In this chapter, we will delve deeper into the workings of the stock market and the factors that affect its performance.

The stock market has various players involved in trading, investing, and regulating the market.

Some of the players include:

1. **THE STOCK EXCHANGE**

    The platform where transactions in shares are executed. Each stock exchange has its rules and regulations whereby listed companies must abide by. This includes general regulations issued by the SEC.

2. **THE SECURITIES & EXCHANGE COMMISSION (SEC)**

    The apex regulatory body overseeing the capital market, with the main job of regulating the capital market with a view to protecting investors and developing the capital market.

3. **CENTRAL OR SETTLEMENT DEPOSITORY**

    This is a central body that tracks all transactions and balances books of companies based on daily stock exchange transactions.

4. **STOCKBROKERS**

Licensed professionals who buy and sell stocks and other securities for both retail and institutional clients through a stock exchange or over the counter in return for a fee or commission. With technology and online trading, investors buy and sell stocks directly in the market using their broker's online trading platforms.

5. **SELLERS**

    Sellers are typically companies or individuals who are selling their shares in the company.

6. **INDIVIDUAL INVESTORS**

    Individuals seeking to invest their savings in the stock market. Individual stock investors can be categorized by income into different groups:

    a) **High Net Worth Individuals (HNWI):** These are individuals with a net worth of at least $1 million, excluding their primary residence. HNWIs are often considered accredited investors and have access to a wider range of investment opportunities, including private equity and hedge funds.

    b) **Mass Affluent:** These are individuals who have a net worth between $100,000 and $1 million or an annual income between $75,000 and $250,000. Mass affluent investors often invest in stocks, bonds, mutual funds, and exchange-traded funds (ETFs).

    c) **Retail Investors:** These are individual investors with a net worth of less than $100,000 and an annual income of less than $75,000. Retail investors usually invest in stocks, bonds, mutual funds, and exchange traded funds (ETFs) through a brokerage account or retirement account such as an IRA or 401(k). They may also use robo-advisors or financial advisors for investment guidance.

    These income categories are not set in stone and may vary depending on the country, region, or financial institution.

7. **INSTITUTIONAL INVESTORS**

   Big players who mobilize funds from the public to invest on their behalf for a fee, including mutual funds, investment houses, and banks.

8. **BANKS**

   Investment banks and discount houses help package private placements and initial public offerings.

   Banks also provide margin loans to high net worth investors to trade. Banks often provide margin loans through brokers. Online stock trading incorporates margin trading, allowing smaller traders with low funds access to the market.

STOCK INDICES

Stock indices are benchmarks used to measure the performance of the stock market or specific segments of the market.

The most widely recognized stock index is the Dow Jones Industrial Average, which tracks the performance of 30 large, publicly traded companies. Other popular indices include the S&P 500, which tracks the performance of 500 large-cap U.S. companies, and the Nasdaq Composite, which tracks the performance of technology stocks.

FACTORS THAT AFFECT THE STOCK MARKET

The stock market is affected by a variety of factors, including:

1. **Company performance**: The performance of individual companies can have a significant impact on the stock market. Good earnings reports and positive news can cause stock prices to rise, while negative news can cause stock prices to fall.

2. **Economic indicators**: Economic indicators such as GDP, inflation rates, and employment data can affect the stock mar-

ket. A strong economy can lead to higher stock prices, while a weak economy can lead to lower stock prices.

3. **Interest rates**: Changes in interest rates can affect the stock market. Lower interest rates can lead to higher stock prices, as investors look for higher returns on their investments.

4. **Global events**: Global events such as political instability, natural disasters, or pandemics can affect the stock market. Negative events can cause stock prices to fall, while positive events can cause stock prices to rise.

5. **Investor sentiment**: Investor sentiment, or how investors feel about the market, can also affect stock prices. Optimistic investors can lead to higher stock prices, while pessimistic investors can lead to lower stock prices.

In the next chapter, we will discuss the different types of individual investors in on the stock market and their characteristics.

4: TYPES OF INDIVIDUAL STOCK INVESTORS

Individual stock investors can be categorized based on their investment objectives and strategies.

Here are some common categories of individual stock investors:

1) GROWTH INVESTORS

These investors focus on buying stocks of companies that are expected to grow at a faster pace than the market or industry average.

They are willing to pay a premium for the stocks with the expectation of significant capital gains in the long run.

2) VALUE INVESTORS

These investors focus on buying stocks that are undervalued by the market and have a potential for appreciation in the future.

They look for companies that have strong fundamentals but are temporarily out of favor or overlooked by the market.

3) INCOME INVESTORS

These investors focus on buying stocks that pay regular dividends or have a history of increasing dividends over time. They look for companies with a stable financial position and consistent cash flow that can support the dividend payments.

4) MOMENTUM INVESTORS

These investors focus on buying stocks that have shown positive momentum in the recent past. They believe that the stocks that have performed well in the past will continue to perform well in the near future.

5) CONTRARIAN INVESTORS

These investors focus on buying stocks that are out of favor or have been beaten down by the market. They believe that the market overreacts to the news and creates buying opportunities in the stocks that are temporarily out of favor.

6) DAY TRADERS

These investors buy and sell stocks frequently within a day to take advantage of short-term price movements. They use technical analysis and trading strategies to make quick profits from the stock market.

7) INDEX INVESTORS

These investors buy and hold a diversified portfolio of stocks that tracks a particular index, such as the S&P 500. They believe that over the long term, the stock market will provide good returns, and they do not try to beat the market by picking individual stocks.

8) SPECULATORS

These investors take on high levels of risk by investing in stocks that have the potential for significant gains but are also highly volatile. They often invest based on rumors, news events, or other speculative factors rather than fundamentals.

Investors may fall into more than one category, and their investment approach may change over time as their goals and risk tolerance change.

In the next chapter, we will discuss the different types of securities that can be traded on the stock market and their characteristics.

5: TYPES OF STOCKS AND STOCK MARKET INDICES

In this chapter, we will discuss the different types of stocks and stock market indices that investors should be familiar with before investing in the stock market.

TYPES OF STOCKS

1. COMMON STOCKS

Common stocks are the most common type of stock that companies issue. These stocks represent ownership in the company and give shareholders the right to vote at shareholder meetings and receive dividends.

2. PREFERRED STOCKS

Preferred stocks have characteristics of both stocks and bonds. They typically pay fixed dividends and have priority over common stocks when it comes to receiving dividends or assets in the event of a company's bankruptcy.

3. BLUE-CHIP STOCKS

Blue-chip stocks are stocks of large, well-established companies with a long history of stable earnings and dividend payments. Examples of blue-chip stocks include Microsoft, Coca-Cola, and Johnson & Johnson.

4. GROWTH STOCKS

Growth stocks are stocks of companies with high growth potential, but may not pay dividends. These companies often reinvest profits back into the company to fuel growth, and investors may see significant capital appreciation if the company performs well.

5. VALUE STOCKS

Value stocks are stocks of companies that are undervalued by the market, either due to short-term problems or overlooked opportunities. Investors in value stocks aim to buy low and sell high when the market recognizes the true value of the company.

STOCK MARKET INDICES

Stock market indices are used to track the performance of the stock market or a specific segment of the market. Here are some of the most well-known stock market indices:

1. S&P 500

The S&P 500 is a market-capitalization-weighted index that tracks the performance of 500 large-cap U.S. companies. It is often used as a benchmark for the overall performance of the U.S. stock market.

2. Dow Jones Industrial Average

The Dow Jones Industrial Average is a price-weighted index that tracks the performance of 30 large, publicly traded companies in various industries.

3. Nasdaq Composite

The Nasdaq Composite is a market-capitalization-weighted index that tracks the performance of over 3,000 companies listed on the Nasdaq stock exchange, primarily technology and growth-oriented companies.

4. **Russell 2000**

The Russell 2000 is a market-capitalization-weighted index that tracks the performance of 2,000 small-cap U.S. companies.

Before investing in the stock market, it is important to understand the different types of stocks and stock market indices. Common and preferred stocks have different characteristics and advantages, while blue-chip, growth, and value stocks offer investors different investment strategies.

Stock market indices provide a benchmark for the performance of the market or a specific segment of the market.

In the next chapter, we will discuss how to evaluate individual stocks and make informed investment decisions.

6: WHY INVEST IN STOCKS?

Before diving into any market, it is important to have clear investment objectives. Are you seeking income, capital appreciation, or both?

INVESTING FOR INCOME

Investing for income involves building a stock portfolio that generates regular dividends. This means purchasing shares from companies that pay dividends on an annual or bi-annual basis.

You earn money by receiving dividends on your shares rather than selling them. This dividend income becomes one of your streams of income. You can keep the shares and gift it to your descendants or sell some of them to raise money for another investment opportunity.

Your income target determines the companies you add to your stock portfolio and the number of shares you need to own.

To maximize your return on investment, it is best to purchase stocks when the prices are low, as this will allow you to get more shares for the same amount of money. Buying low also means you can expect a higher and faster return on investment, making it a long-term investment strategy.

Investing for income allows you to build wealth, as your net worth increases with the value of your shares. Most of the billionaires in the Forbes list get their through the value of share in companies they own.

INVESTING FOR CAPITAL GAIN

Investing for capital gain, on the other hand, means making money by buying stocks at a low price and selling them when their prices increase. Your profit comes from the capital gain, which is the difference between the selling and cost price.

To implement this strategy, you need to look for stocks with the potential for price appreciation and purchase them while the prices are still low.

You also need to understand market trends, to know when to buy when prices are low, and when to sell when prices crest.

Investing for capital gain is a short-term strategy which exposed you to the twin emotions of fear and greed. Fear of loss may lead to premature selling when prices crash (bear market) while greed for gain may lead to buying overpriced stocks when prices boom (bull market).

This is not a long-term investment strategy, but rather a stock trading strategy.

***

Your financial goal will determine which stocks you should buy, how many you should buy, and when to sell them.

It is also important to understand asset allocation and the role that stocks play in your financial portfolio. If you do not have a regular income, your focus should be investing for income, which includes fixed income investments, including companies that pay regular dividends.

Income from stocks is not always predictable, as a company that performed well one year may not perform as well the next. Therefore, income from stock market investments can fluctuate.

Many investors switch between the stock market and the money market, fleeing to the stock market when the money market yields drop and returning to the money market when yields rise.

While this may seem like a smart move, it may not be the best overall strategy. Each market has a specific role in your financial portfolio and should be viewed on a long-term basis. A stock market crash may actually be a buying opportunity for a savvy investor rather than a signal to flee to the safety of the money market.

If you are investing for income, it does not matter whether the market is booming or crashing, as long as your dividend income comes in as expected. A market crash provides an opportunity to purchase more stocks and expand your portfolio.

On the other hand, if you are investing for capital gain, a market crash also presents a chance to purchase stocks at a discount and hold on to them until the market recovers before selling.

It is important to note that if you invest in solid companies, it will not matter what the market is doing – you will always receive good value for your investment.

7: HOW SAFE ARE STOCKS?

When it comes to investing, one of the most common questions is: how safe are stocks? While there is no simple answer to this question, there are a number of factors that can impact the safety of investing in stocks.

Let's explore the risks of investing in stocks, as well as the factors that can impact the safety of your investments.

THE RISKS OF INVESTING IN STOCKS

One of the biggest risks of investing in stocks is the potential for loss. Unlike bonds or other fixed-income investments, stocks do not guarantee a return on your investment. Instead, the value of your stocks will fluctuate based on a variety of factors, including market conditions, company performance, and economic trends.

Additionally, individual stocks can be subject to a variety of risks, such as poor management, competitive threats, and regulatory changes. If a company experiences financial difficulties or fails altogether, investors may lose some or all of their investment in that stock.

Another risk of investing in stocks is volatility. The stock market is known for its ups and downs, and sudden drops in stock prices can be unsettling for investors.

However, it's important to remember that volatility is a normal part of investing in stocks, and that over the long term, the stock market has historically provided strong returns.

FACTORS THAT IMPACT THE SAFETY OF STOCKS

While investing in stocks carries risks, there are a number of factors that can impact the safety of your investments. These include:

1. DIVERSIFICATION

One of the key ways to reduce risk when investing in stocks is to diversify your portfolio. By investing in a variety of different stocks across different industries and sectors, you can spread your risk and potentially minimize losses if one sector or industry experiences a downturn.

2. COMPANY FUNDAMENTALS

When investing in individual stocks, it's important to evaluate the fundamentals of the company. This includes factors such as the company's financial health, management team, and competitive position within its industry.

Companies with strong fundamentals are generally considered to be safer investments, as they are better positioned to weather economic downturns and industry disruptions.

3. MARKET TRENDS

The broader market can also impact the safety of investing in stocks. During periods of economic expansion, stocks tend to perform well, while during economic downturns, stocks may experience significant losses.

By staying informed about market trends and economic indicators, investors can make informed investment decisions and adjust their strategies accordingly.

4. TIME HORIZON

Another factor that can impact the safety of investing in stocks is your time horizon. Investing in stocks is generally considered a long-term strategy, as it can take time for the value of your investments to appreciate.

If you have a shorter time horizon, such as a few years, investing in stocks may carry more risk, as sudden market downturns can impact the value of your investments in the short term.

8: FUNDAMENTAL STOCK INVESTING

Fundamental stock investing is a fundamental approach to investing that involves evaluating a company's financial health and other qualitative factors to determine its intrinsic value and potential for growth.

We will explore the basics of fundamental analysis, including the tools and techniques used, as well as the advantages and limitations of this approach.

WHAT IS FUNDAMENTAL ANALYSIS?

Fundamental analysis is a method of evaluating securities based on the company's financial health and other qualitative factors. This includes analyzing financial statements, such as balance sheets, income statements, and cash flow statements, to determine a company's revenue, expenses, and profitability.

Fundamental analysts also look at other factors, such as the company's management team, market share, and competitive landscape, to determine its long-term potential for growth and profitability.

Tools and Techniques Used in Fundamental Analysis There are a variety of tools and techniques used in fundamental analysis. Here are some of the most common:

a) FINANCIAL STATEMENTS

Fundamental analysts use financial statements, such as balance sheets, income statements, and cash flow statements, to evaluate a company's financial health and performance.

A balance sheet is a financial statement that shows a company's assets, liabilities, and equity at a specific point in time. It provides a snapshot of the company's financial position by showing what the company owns (assets), what it owes (liabilities), and what is left over for the owners (equity).

The balance sheet equation is Assets = Liabilities + Equity.

An income statement is a financial statement that shows a company's revenue, expenses, and net income over a specific period, such as a quarter or a year. It provides information about the company's profitability by showing how much revenue it earned and how much it spent to generate that revenue.

The income statement equation is Revenue - Expenses = Net Income.

A cash flow statement is a financial statement that shows the inflows and outflows of cash and cash equivalents over a specific period. It provides information about the company's liquidity and cash position by showing where its cash is coming from and how it is being used.

The cash flow statement equation is Cash inflows - Cash outflows = Net cash flow.

b) **RATIOS**

Analysts also use financial ratios, such as price-to-earnings (P/E) ratio, price-to-sales (P/S) ratio, and debt-to-equity ratio, to evaluate a company's valuation and financial health.

Price-to-earnings (P/E) ratio is a financial metric that measures the relative value of a company's stock price to its earnings per share (EPS). It is calculated by dividing the current market price per share by the earnings per share.

Price-to-sales (P/S) ratio is a financial metric that measures the relative value of a company's stock price to its sales per share. It is calculated by dividing the current market price per share by the sales per share.

Debt-to-equity ratio is a financial metric that measures the relative amount of debt and equity a company is using to finance its operations. It is calculated by dividing the total liabilities of a company by its shareholders' equity.

c) MANAGEMENT AND INDUSTRY ANALYSIS

Fundamental analysts look at a company's management team, corporate governance, and industry trends to determine its potential for growth and profitability.

d) QUALITATIVE FACTORS

Fundamental analysts also consider other qualitative factors, such as brand reputation, market share, and competitive landscape, when evaluating a company's long-term potential.

ADVANTAGES OF FUNDAMENTAL ANALYSIS

There are several advantages to using fundamental analysis in stock investing:

(i) **Long-Term Focus**: Fundamental analysis is a long-term approach to investing, focused on a company's long-term potential for growth and profitability.

(ii) **Comprehensive**: Fundamental analysis evaluates a wide range of factors, including financial health, management, industry trends, and competitive landscape, to determine a company's intrinsic value.

(iii) **Objective**: Fundamental analysis is a largely objective approach to investing, based on quantitative analysis of financial statements and other data.

(iv) **Widely Used**: Fundamental analysis is a popular approach to investing, and there are many resources available to investors who want to learn more.

Limitations of Fundamental Analysis Despite its advantages, fundamental analysis has some limitations. Here are some of the key limitations:

Time-Consuming

Fundamental analysis can be a time-consuming process, requiring careful evaluation of financial statements and other qualitative factors.

Limited Scope

Fundamental analysis focuses primarily on a company's financial health and other qualitative factors, and does not consider other factors that may impact the stock market, such as geopolitical events or changes in interest rates.

Subjective

Fundamental analysis is not entirely objective, as different analysts may interpret the same data in different ways.

Uncertainty

There is always some degree of uncertainty when it comes to investing, and even the most comprehensive fundamental analysis cannot predict future market movements with certainty.

While there are several advantages to using fundamental analysis, it's important for investors to understand its limitations and use it in conjunction with other types of analysis, such as technical analysis. With the right approach and mindset, fundamental analysis can be a valuable tool for investors looking to make informed investment decisions.

9: TECHNICAL STOCK INVESTING

Technical stock investing, also known as technical analysis, is a popular approach to investing that involves analyzing past market data to identify patterns and predict future price movements.

In this chapter, we'll explore the basics of technical analysis, including the tools and techniques used, as well as the advantages and limitations of this approach.

WHAT IS TECHNICAL ANALYSIS?

Technical analysis is a method of evaluating securities based on statistical analysis of past market data, primarily price and volume. Technical analysts believe that market trends, price patterns, and other technical indicators can provide insight into future price movements.

Technical analysts typically use charts and graphs to visualize past price movements and identify patterns. They may also use technical indicators, such as moving averages or relative strength index (RSI), to identify trends and potential buying or selling opportunities.

Technical analysis is often used in conjunction with other types of analysis, such as fundamental analysis, which focuses on a company's financial health and other qualitative factors.

Tools and Techniques Used in Technical Analysis There are a variety of tools and techniques used in technical analysis. Here are some of the most common:

Chart pattern with indicator. Image: investopedia.com

1. **CHART PATTERNS**

   Technical analysts use chart patterns to identify trends and potential price movements. Common chart patterns include head and shoulders, double tops and bottoms, and triangles.

2. **TECHNICAL INDICATORS**

   Technical indicators are mathematical calculations based on market data. Examples of technical indicators include moving averages, relative strength index (RSI), and stochastic oscillators.

3. **CANDLESTICK CHARTS**

   Candlestick charts provide a visual representation of price movements and are often used in technical analysis. Each candlestick represents a period of time (e.g. a day or an hour) and shows the opening and closing prices, as well as the high and low prices.

4. **VOLUME**

Technical analysts often look at trading volume, or the number of shares traded during a given period, to confirm price movements and identify potential trends.

ADVANTAGES OF TECHNICAL ANALYSIS

There are several advantages to using technical analysis in stock investing:

(i) **Objective**: Technical analysis is a largely objective approach to investing, based on statistical analysis of past market data.

(ii) **Timing**: Technical analysis can help investors identify short-term trends and potential buying or selling opportunities.

(iii) **Easy to Use**: Technical analysis is relatively easy to learn and can be used by investors of all skill levels.

(iv) **Widely Used**: Technical analysis is a popular approach to investing, and there are many resources available to investors who want to learn more.

LIMITATIONS OF TECHNICAL ANALYSIS

Despite its advantages, technical analysis has some limitations. Here are some of the key limitations:

Limited Scope

Technical analysis focuses on past market data and does not consider other factors that may impact the stock market, such as geopolitical events or changes in interest rates.

Subjective

Technical analysis is not entirely objective, as different analysts may interpret the same data in different ways.

Over-Reliance on Indicators

Some investors may rely too heavily on technical indicators and overlook other important factors, such as company fundamentals.

Also, breaking political or market news may cause the market to move in a different direction as indicated.

Lagging Indicators

Some technical indicators are lagging indicators, meaning that they reflect past price movements rather than predicting future ones.

While there are several advantages to using technical analysis, it's important for investors to understand its limitations and use it in conjunction with other types of analysis, such as fundamental analysis. With the right approach and mindset, technical analysis can be a valuable tool for investors looking to make informed investment decisions.

10: HOW TO READ STOCK CHARTS

In this chapter, we will discuss the basics of how to read stock charts. Understanding stock charts is an essential skill for investors who want to make informed investment decisions.

1. TYPES OF STOCK CHARTS

There are three main types of stock charts: line charts, bar charts, and candlestick charts. Each chart displays the same data in a different format.

Line Charts

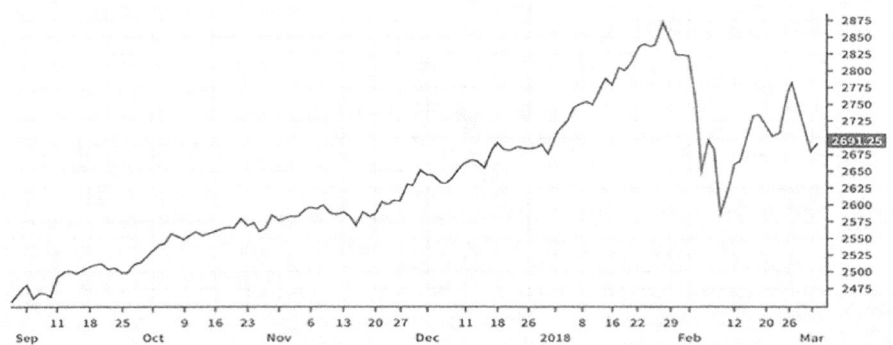

Example of a Line Chart. Image: investopedia.com

Line charts display the closing price of a stock over a period.

They are useful for identifying long-term trends in a stock's price.

Bar Charts

10: HOW TO READ STOCK CHARTS | 33

Example of a Bar Chart. Image: tradingview.com

Bar charts display the high, low, and closing prices of a stock over a period.

They are useful for identifying the volatility of a stock's price. Taller bars indicate higher volatility

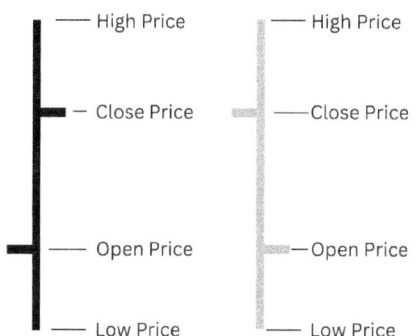

Candlestick Charts

34 | STOCK MARKET INVESTING 101

Example of a Candlestick Chart. Image: metatrader4.com

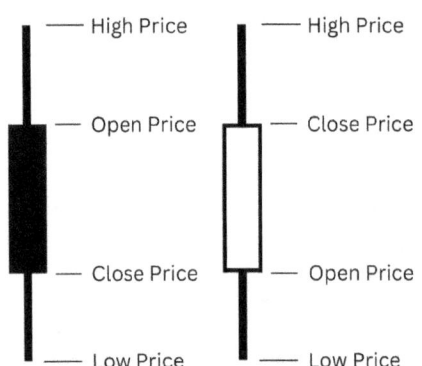

Candlestick charts display the opening, closing, high, and low prices of a stock over a period.

Candlestick charts originated in Japan over 100 years before the West developed the bar and point-and-figure charts.

They are useful for identifying price trends and market sentiment and volatility (based on height of candle).

2. TIMEFRAMES

Stock charts can be viewed in different timeframes, such as daily, weekly, or monthly. Investors should select a timeframe that aligns with their investment goals and strategies. For example, a long-term investor may prefer to view charts in monthly or yearly intervals, while a short-term trader may prefer to view charts in hourly or daily intervals.

3. INDICATORS

Indicators are tools used to analyze stock charts and identify trends. There are many different types of indicators, including moving averages, relative strength index (RSI), and Bollinger Bands. Investors should familiarize themselves with different indicators and use them to supplement their analysis of stock charts.

4. SUPPORT AND RESISTANCE

Support and resistance levels are important concepts in technical analysis. Support refers to a price level at which buying pressure is strong enough to prevent a stock from declining further, while resistance refers to a price level at which selling pressure is strong enough to prevent a stock from rising further. These levels can be identified by analyzing stock charts and can be used to inform buying and selling decisions.

5. VOLUME

Volume is the number of shares traded in a stock over a period of time. High volume can indicate strong investor interest in a stock, while low volume can indicate weak investor interest. Investors should pay attention to volume when analyzing stock charts.

Reading stock charts is an important skill for investors who want to make informed investment decisions. There are different types of stock charts, each displaying the same data in a different format. Investors should select a timeframe that aligns with their investment goals and strategies, and use indicators, support and resistance levels, and volume to analyze stock charts.

In the next chapter, we will discuss how to evaluate a company's financial health before investing in its stock.

11: EVALUATING COMPANIES AND STOCKS

In this chapter, we will discuss how to evaluate companies and stocks before making investment decisions. It is important for investors to thoroughly understand the financial health of a company before investing in its stock.

1. FINANCIAL STATEMENTS

The financial statements of a company provide a snapshot of its financial health. The three main financial statements are the balance sheet, income statement, and cash flow statement. Investors should review these statements to assess a company's profitability, liquidity, and solvency.

Balance Sheet

The balance sheet provides a snapshot of a company's assets, liabilities, and equity at a specific point in time. It shows how much a company owns (assets) and how much it owes (liabilities), as well as the value of its shareholders' equity. Investors should look at a company's balance sheet to assess its liquidity and solvency.

Income Statement

The income statement shows a company's revenue, expenses, and profits over a specific period of time. It provides an overview of a company's profitability. Investors should look at a company's income statement to assess its revenue growth and profit margins.

Cash Flow Statement

The cash flow statement shows a company's cash inflows and outflows over a specific period of time. It provides insight into a company's liquidity and cash management. Investors should look at a company's cash flow statement to assess its ability to generate cash and meet its financial obligations.

2. FINANCIAL RATIOS

Financial ratios are calculations that compare different financial metrics to provide insight into a company's financial health. There are many different financial ratios, but some of the most important ones include:

Price-to-Earnings Ratio (P/E Ratio)

The P/E ratio compares a company's stock price to its earnings per share. It is a measure of how much investors are willing to pay for each dollar of earnings. A high P/E ratio can indicate that a stock is overvalued, while a low P/E ratio can indicate that a stock is undervalued.

Price-to-Sales Ratio (P/S Ratio)

The P/S ratio compares a company's stock price to its revenue per share. It is a measure of how much investors are willing to pay for each dollar of revenue. A high P/S ratio can indicate that a stock is overvalued, while a low P/S ratio can indicate that a stock is undervalued.

Return on Equity (ROE)

ROE measures a company's profitability by comparing its net income to its shareholder equity. It is a measure of how efficiently a company is using its shareholders' equity to generate profits.

3. INDUSTRY ANALYSIS

Investors should also conduct industry analysis to assess the competitive landscape and growth potential of a company's industry. This can help investors identify opportunities and risks associated with investing in a particular company. Investors should look at industry trends, competitors, and regulatory developments to inform their investment decisions.

Evaluating companies and stocks is an essential part of making informed investment decisions. Investors should review a company's financial statements and financial ratios to assess its financial health. They should also conduct industry analysis to assess the competitive landscape and growth potential of a company's industry.

In the next chapter, we will discuss how to build a diversified investment portfolio.

12: RISK MANAGEMENT STRATEGIES

Investing in the stock market involves taking risks, but there are ways to manage those risks to help protect your investments. In this chapter, we will discuss some risk management strategies that investors can use to help minimize their exposure to potential losses.

1. DIVERSIFICATION

One of the most important risk management strategies is diversification. This means spreading your investments across different types of assets, sectors, and geographic regions to help reduce the impact of market volatility on your portfolio. Diversification can help you avoid putting all your eggs in one basket, and it can help you manage risk over the long term.

2. ASSET ALLOCATION

Asset allocation is another important risk management strategy. This involves dividing your investments among different asset classes, such as stocks, bonds, and cash. Each asset class has its own level of risk and return, so asset allocation can help you balance risk and return in your portfolio.

For example, if you are a conservative investor, you may want to allocate a larger portion of your portfolio to bonds and cash, which are generally less risky than stocks.

3. STOP LOSS ORDERS

Stop loss orders are another risk management strategy that investors can use to help minimize potential losses. A stop loss order is an order to sell a stock when it reaches a certain price point. This can help you limit your losses if a stock's price starts to fall.

For example, if you buy a stock at $50 per share, you may set a stop loss order at $45 per share. If the stock's price falls to $45 per share, the stop loss order will automatically sell the stock, helping you limit your potential losses.

4. DOLLAR-COST AVERAGING

Dollar-cost averaging is a risk management strategy that involves investing a fixed amount of money at regular intervals over a period of time. This can help you avoid the risk of investing a large amount of money at a single point in time when the market may be at a high point. By investing a fixed amount of money at regular intervals, you can average out your purchase price over time and potentially reduce your exposure to market volatility.

5. RESEARCH AND DUE DILIGENCE

One of the most important risk management strategies is to conduct thorough research and due diligence before making any investment decisions. This means reviewing a company's financial statements, analyzing its industry and competitive landscape, and understanding the potential risks and opportunities associated with the investment. By conducting thorough research, you can help reduce the risk of investing in companies that may not be financially stable or that may not have strong growth potential.

Investing in the stock market involves taking risks, but there are ways to manage those risks to help protect your investments. Diversification, asset allocation, stop loss orders, dollar-cost averaging, and research and due diligence are all important risk management strategies that investors can use to help minimize their exposure to potential losses.

By incorporating these strategies into your investment plan, you can help manage risk and potentially improve your long-term investment returns.

13: DEVELOPING A STOCK INVESTING PLAN

Investing in the stock market can be a daunting task, but developing a stock investing plan can help you stay focused and achieve your investment goals. In this chapter, we will discuss the key components of a stock investing plan and provide some tips on how to create a plan that works for you.

1. DEFINE YOUR INVESTMENT GOALS

The first step in developing a stock investing plan is to define your investment goals. This could include things like saving for retirement, funding a child's education, or building wealth over the long term. Once you have a clear understanding of your investment goals, you can develop a plan that aligns with your objectives.

2. DETERMINE YOUR RISK TOLERANCE

Your risk tolerance is an important factor to consider when developing a stock investing plan. Some investors are comfortable taking on higher levels of risk in exchange for the potential for higher returns, while others prefer a more conservative approach. Understanding your risk tolerance can help you make investment decisions that align with your comfort level.

3. CHOOSE YOUR INVESTMENT STRATEGY

There are many different investment strategies to choose from when investing in the stock market. Some investors prefer a passive approach, such as investing in index funds or exchange-traded funds (ETFs), while others prefer a more active approach, such as investing in individual stocks or actively managed mutual funds. Your investment strategy should align with your investment goals and risk tolerance.

4. SELECT YOUR INVESTMENTS

Once you have a clear understanding of your investment goals, risk tolerance, and investment strategy, you can begin selecting your investments. This could include individual stocks, mutual funds, ETFs, or other investment vehicles. It's important to conduct thorough research and due diligence on each investment to ensure that it aligns with your investment goals and risk tolerance.

5. MONITOR AND ADJUST YOUR PLAN

Investing in the stock market is not a set-it-and-forget-it process. It's important to regularly monitor your investments and adjust your plan as needed to ensure that it remains aligned with your investment goals and risk tolerance. This could include rebalancing your portfolio, adjusting your investment strategy, or making changes to your investment holdings.

Developing a stock investing plan can help you stay focused on your investment goals and make informed investment decisions. Key components of a stock investing plan include defining your investment goals, determining your risk tolerance, choosing your investment strategy, selecting your investments, and monitoring and adjusting your plan over time.

By following these steps and staying disciplined, you can potentially achieve your investment goals and build long-term wealth through stock market investing.

14: DIFFERENT WAYS TO INVEST IN THE STOCK MARKET

Investing in the stock market can be done in various ways. In this chapter, we will discuss some of the most common ways to invest in the stock market and their advantages and disadvantages.

1. INDIVIDUAL STOCKS

Individual stocks are shares of a single company that can be purchased on a stock exchange. Investing in individual stocks can provide the potential for high returns, but it also carries a higher level of risk. When investing in individual stocks, it's important to conduct thorough research on the company and its financial performance.

Advantages

Potential for high returns, ability to invest in specific companies that align with personal values or interests.

Disadvantages

Higher risk, potential for loss of capital, requires time and expertise to research and select individual stocks.

2. MUTUAL FUNDS

Mutual funds are investment vehicles that pool money from multiple investors to purchase a diversified portfolio of stocks, bonds, or other assets.

Mutual funds are managed by professional fund managers who

select the investments based on the fund's investment objective. Investing in mutual funds can provide diversification and professional management, but it also carries fees and expenses.

Advantages

Diversification, professional management, access to a variety of investment strategies and asset classes.

Disadvantages

Fees and expenses, potential for underperformance compared to the market, limited control over the selection of individual investments.

3. EXCHANGE-TRADED FUNDS (ETFs)

ETFs are similar to mutual funds in that they provide diversification through a portfolio of investments, but they trade like individual stocks on an exchange.

ETFs can be bought and sold throughout the trading day, and they typically have lower fees and expenses than mutual funds.

Advantages

Diversification, lower fees and expenses than mutual funds, flexibility to trade throughout the day.

Disadvantages

Potential for underperformance compared to the market, limited control over the selection of individual investments.

4. INDEX FUNDS

Index funds are a type of mutual fund or ETF that tracks a specific stock market index, such as the S&P 500 or the Dow Jones Industrial Average. Index funds provide broad market exposure and are typically low-cost, making them a popular choice for passive investors.

Advantages

Broad market exposure, low fees and expenses, passive investment approach.

Disadvantages

Limited control over the selection of individual investments, potential for underperformance compared to the market.

There are various ways to invest in the stock market, each with its own advantages and disadvantages. Investing in individual stocks can provide the potential for high returns, but it also carries a higher level of risk. Mutual funds, ETFs, and index funds provide diversification and professional management, but they also carry fees and expenses.

When selecting an investment strategy, it's important to consider personal investment goals, risk tolerance, and time horizon.

15: ONLINE AND OFFLINE STOCK TRADING

With advancements in technology, investors now have the option to trade stocks both online and offline. In this chapter, we will discuss the differences between online and offline stock trading and the advantages and disadvantages of each.

1. ONLINE STOCK TRADING

Online stock trading allows investors to buy and sell stocks through a trading platform provided by an online brokerage.

Online trading platforms offer real-time market data, research tools, and easy access to trading, making it a popular choice for investors. Online trading can also be done through mobile apps, allowing investors to trade on-the-go.

Advantages

Easy access to trading, real-time market data, research tools, lower fees and commissions, convenient.

Disadvantages

Potential for internet connectivity issues, reliance on technology, lack of personal interaction with a broker.

2. OFFLINE STOCK TRADING

Offline stock trading, also known as traditional or full-service brokerage, involves working with a broker to buy and sell stocks.

Brokers provide personalized investment advice, research reports, and can help with trade execution. Offline trading typically involves higher fees and commissions than online trading.

Advantages

Personalized investment advice, research reports, trade execution assistance, potential for better pricing on trades.

Disadvantages

Higher fees and commissions, limited access to real-time market data, less convenient than online trading.

3. HYBRID TRADING

Hybrid trading combines elements of both online and offline trading.

This allows investors to benefit from the convenience and lower fees of online trading while also having access to personalized investment advice and trade execution assistance from a broker.

Advantages

Lower fees and commissions than full-service brokerage, personalized investment advice, access to real-time market data, convenient.

Disadvantages

Potential for higher fees than online trading, limited personal interaction with a broker.

***

Both online and offline trading have their advantages and disadvantages.

Online trading is convenient and typically involves lower fees, but can be reliant on technology and lacks personal interaction with a broker.

Offline trading provides personalized investment advice and trade execution assistance, but typically involves higher fees and commissions.

Hybrid trading allows investors to benefit from both approaches, but can come with higher fees than online trading. Ultimately, the choice between online and offline trading depends on personal preference and investment goals.

16: CHOOSING A BROKERAGE

When it comes to investing in the stock market, choosing the right brokerage can have a significant impact on your investment experience. A reliable method for choosing a broker is to seek recommendations from trustworthy and knowledgeable acquaintances, such as friends, family, or colleagues.

However, even with a recommendation, it's advisable to follow the conventional wisdom of "trust but verify."

In this chapter, we will discuss the factors you should consider when choosing a brokerage.

1. FEES AND COMMISSIONS

One of the most important factors to consider when choosing a brokerage is the fees and commissions they charge. Some brokerages charge a flat fee per trade, while others charge a percentage of the trade value.

Additionally, some brokerages may charge account maintenance fees or other hidden fees. Be sure to compare the fees and commissions of different brokerages to find one that aligns with your investment budget.

2. TRADING PLATFORM AND TOOLS

The trading platform and tools provided by a brokerage can also impact your investment experience. Look for a brokerage that offers a user-friendly trading platform with real-time market data and research tools. Some brokerages also offer educational resources and investment research reports to help you make informed investment decisions.

3. CUSTOMER SERVICE AND SUPPORT

Customer service and support are essential when it comes to investing in the stock market. Look for a brokerage that provides responsive customer support through multiple channels, such as phone, email, and live chat. Some brokerages also offer personal account managers or financial advisors who can provide personalized investment advice.

4. INVESTMENT PRODUCTS

The investment products offered by a brokerage can also impact your investment experience. Look for a brokerage that offers a wide range of investment products, including stocks, bonds, mutual funds, and ETFs. Additionally, consider whether the brokerage offers access to international markets or alternative investments.

5. WALKING THE TALK

When seeking investment guidance for your stock portfolio, it's crucial to opt for a brokerage with brokers who are personally invested in the market - individuals with "skin in the game." Be wary of someone who offers advice but has no personal stake in the matter, as it may not align with your best interests.

As famously stated by Warren Buffet, *"Wall Street is the only place that people ride to in a Rolls Royce to get advice from those who take the subway."*

6. SECURITY AND REGULATION

Finally, consider the security and regulation of the brokerage you are considering. Look for a brokerage that is regulated by a reputable regulatory body, such as the Securities and Exchange Commission (SEC). Additionally, look for a brokerage that uses industry-standard security measures, such as encryption and two-factor authentication, to protect your personal and financial information.

Choosing the right brokerage is essential for a successful investment experience. Consider factors such as fees and commissions, trading platform and tools, customer service and support, investment products, and security and regulation when choosing a brokerage.

Be sure to compare multiple brokerages to find one that aligns with your investment goals and budget.

17: OPENING AND MANAGING A BROKERAGE ACCOUNT

Once you have chosen a brokerage that aligns with your investment goals and budget, it's time to open a brokerage account. In this chapter, we will discuss the steps to open and manage a brokerage account.

1. **GATHER REQUIRED INFORMATION**

    To open a brokerage account, you will need to provide personal information such as your name, address, date of birth, and Social Security number. You may also need to provide financial information, such as your employment status, income, and net worth. Additionally, you will need to provide information about your investment goals and risk tolerance.

2. **CHOOSE THE TYPE OF ACCOUNT**

    The next step is to choose the type of brokerage account you want to open. Common types of brokerage accounts include individual brokerage accounts, joint brokerage accounts, and retirement accounts such as IRAs and 401(k)s. Be sure to choose the account type that aligns with your investment goals and needs.

3. **FUND YOUR ACCOUNT**

    Once you have opened your brokerage account, you will need to fund it. Most brokerages offer several funding options, such as bank transfers, wire transfers, or credit/debit card payments. Be sure to consider any fees associated with each funding option before choosing one.

4. PLACE TRADES AND MANAGE YOUR PORTFOLIO

Once your account is funded, you can begin placing trades and managing your portfolio. Most brokerages offer a user-friendly trading platform that allows you to buy and sell stocks, bonds, mutual funds, ETFs, and other investment products. Additionally, most brokerages provide portfolio management tools and investment research to help you make informed investment decisions.

5. MONITOR YOUR ACCOUNT AND MAKE ADJUSTMENTS

Finally, it's important to monitor your brokerage account regularly and make adjustments as needed. Monitor your account performance and track your investments to ensure they align with your investment goals and risk tolerance. Additionally, be sure to keep your personal and financial information up to date with your brokerage.

Opening and managing a brokerage account is an essential step in investing in the stock market. Be sure to gather the required information, choose the type of account that aligns with your investment goals, fund your account, place trades and manage your portfolio, and monitor your account regularly.

With the right brokerage and account management, you can achieve your investment goals and build wealth over time.

18: PLACING TRADES AND EXECUTING ORDERS

Once you have opened and funded a brokerage account, you can begin placing trades and executing orders to buy and sell stocks and other securities. In this chapter, we will discuss the basics of placing trades and executing orders.

1. CHOOSE THE TYPE OF ORDER

Before placing a trade, you need to choose the type of order you want to use. Common types of orders include market orders, limit orders, stop orders, and trailing stop orders. Each type of order has its advantages and disadvantages, so be sure to choose the one that aligns with your investment goals and risk tolerance.

2. ENTER TRADE DETAILS

After choosing the type of order, you need to enter the trade details. This includes the stock symbol, the number of shares you want to buy or sell, and the price you are willing to pay or receive. Be sure to double-check the trade details before submitting the order.

3. REVIEW AND SUBMIT ORDER

Once you have entered the trade details, review them to ensure they are accurate. If everything looks good, submit the order. Your broker will execute the trade on your behalf.

4. MONITOR ORDER STATUS

After submitting the order, you can monitor its status. Most brokerages provide real-time order status updates, so you can see when the order is filled or cancelled.

5. MANAGE YOUR OPEN ORDERS

If your order is not immediately filled, it becomes an open order. You can manage open orders by cancelling or modifying them. Be sure to monitor your open orders regularly to ensure they align with your investment goals and risk tolerance.

6. BE MINDFUL OF TRADING FEES

Finally, be mindful of trading fees when placing trades and executing orders. Most brokerages charge a commission or a per-trade fee, so be sure to factor this into your trading strategy.

Placing trades and executing orders is a crucial part of investing in the stock market. Be sure to choose the type of order that aligns with your investment goals, enter accurate trade details, review and submit the order, monitor its status, manage your open orders, and be mindful of trading fees.

With the right trading strategy and execution, you can achieve your investment goals and build wealth over time.

19: MARKET ORDERS, LIMIT ORDERS, AND STOP ORDERS

When it comes to placing trades and executing orders, there are several types of orders to choose from. In this chapter, we will discuss the most commonly used order types: market orders, limit orders, and stop orders.

1. MARKET ORDERS

A market order is an order to buy or sell a stock at the current market price. Market orders are executed immediately, so you are guaranteed to buy or sell the stock, but the price may not be exactly what you wanted. Market orders are typically used when you need to buy or sell a stock quickly, and the exact price is not as important as getting the trade executed.

2. LIMIT ORDERS

A limit order is an order to buy or sell a stock at a specific price or better. When you place a limit order, you specify the maximum price you are willing to pay for a stock (if you are buying) or the minimum price you are willing to sell it for (if you are selling). The order will only be executed if the stock reaches the specified price or better. Limit orders can help you control the price you pay for a stock, but there is no guarantee that the order will be filled.

3. STOP ORDERS

A stop order is an order to buy or sell a stock once it reaches a certain price. Stop orders are often used as a risk management tool to limit losses or protect profits. If you own a stock and want to limit your losses, you can place a stop order to sell the stock if it drops to a certain price.

If you are short-selling a stock, you can place a stop order to buy it back if the stock rises to a certain price. Stop orders are executed as market orders, so there is no guarantee that you will receive the exact price you specified.

4. OTHER ORDER TYPES

There are other order types that you can use, such as stop-limit orders and trailing stop orders. A stop-limit order is a combination of a stop order and a limit order. It specifies a stop price and a limit price. If the stock reaches the stop price, the order becomes a limit order, and it will only be executed if the stock reaches the limit price.

A trailing stop order is a type of stop order that is based on a percentage or dollar amount. The stop price is set a certain percentage or dollar amount below the current market price, and it moves up as the market price rises.

Market orders, limit orders, and stop orders are the most commonly used order types in stock trading. Each type of order has its advantages and disadvantages, so it's important to choose the one that aligns with your investment goals and risk tolerance.

Remember to review and double-check the order details before submitting the order, and monitor its status to ensure it aligns with your investment strategy.

With the right order type and execution, you can achieve your investment goals and build wealth over time.

20: STRATEGIES FOR STOCK MARKET INVESTING

Investing in the stock market can be both exciting and daunting. While there are no guarantees in investing, there are strategies that you can use to increase your chances of success.

In this chapter, we will discuss some of the most popular strategies for stock market investing.

1. VALUE INVESTING

Value investing is a strategy that involves finding stocks that are undervalued by the market. This involves looking for stocks that have a lower price-to-earnings ratio (P/E ratio) or a lower price-to-book ratio (P/B ratio) than their peers in the same industry.

Value investors believe that the market has overlooked these stocks and that they have the potential for growth in the future.

2. GROWTH INVESTING

Growth investing is a strategy that focuses on investing in stocks that have high potential for growth. This involves looking for stocks in companies that are expected to have high revenue and earnings growth rates in the future. Growth investors believe that these companies will outperform the market over time.

3. INCOME INVESTING

Income investing is a strategy that focuses on investing in stocks that pay a high dividend yield. This involves looking for stocks in companies that have a history of paying and increasing their dividends over time. Income investors believe that these stocks provide a steady stream of income and can also provide some capital appreciation over time.

4. INDEX INVESTING

Index investing is a strategy that involves investing in a broad market index, such as the S&P 500. This provides exposure to a diversified portfolio of stocks and can help reduce the risk of individual stock picks. Index investors believe that the market as a whole will outperform individual stocks over time.

5. MOMENTUM INVESTING

Momentum investing is a strategy that involves investing in stocks that have shown positive trends in price and performance. This involves looking for stocks that have had recent price increases or higher trading volumes. Momentum investors believe that these stocks will continue to perform well in the future.

6. DOLLAR-COST AVERAGING

Dollar-cost averaging is a strategy that involves investing a fixed amount of money into a stock or portfolio on a regular basis, regardless of the market conditions. This helps to reduce the impact of market volatility on your portfolio and can provide a disciplined approach to investing over time.

There are many different strategies for stock market investing, and the best one for you will depend on your investment goals, risk tolerance, and personal preferences. It's important to do your research, diversify your portfolio, and monitor your investments regularly.

With the right strategy and mindset, you can achieve your investment goals and build wealth over time.

21: LONG-TERM AND SHORT-TERM INVESTING

When it comes to investing in the stock market, there are two main approaches: long-term investing and short-term investing. In this chapter, we will discuss the differences between these two approaches and the benefits and drawbacks of each.

LONG-TERM INVESTING

Long-term investing is a strategy that involves holding onto investments for an extended period, typically five years or longer. The primary goal of long-term investing is to build wealth gradually over time, rather than trying to make quick profits.

Long-term investors often choose stocks that have a strong track record of growth and are expected to continue to perform well in the future.

One of the key benefits of long-term investing is that it can help reduce the impact of market volatility on your portfolio. While short-term price fluctuations may cause panic and lead to rash investment decisions, a long-term investor can weather these ups and downs and stay focused on their goals.

Another advantage of long-term investing is that it allows you to take advantage of the power of compounding. Over time, your investments can grow exponentially as your earnings are reinvested into your portfolio.

SHORT-TERM INVESTING

Short-term investing, also known as trading, is a strategy that involves buying and selling investments within a relatively short period, typically less than one year. The primary goal of short-term investing is to make quick profits by taking advantage of market fluctuations.

One of the main benefits of short-term investing is that it can generate higher returns in a shorter amount of time. Short-term investors often look for stocks that have recently experienced a dip in price or are expected to rise in the near future.

However, short-term investing can be risky, as it requires making quick decisions based on limited information. Short-term investors also face higher transaction costs and taxes, which can eat into their profits.

CHOOSING THE RIGHT APPROACH

When it comes to choosing between long-term and short-term investing, there is no one-size-fits-all approach. Your decision will depend on your investment goals, risk tolerance, and personal preferences.

If you are investing for retirement or other long-term goals, long-term investing is generally the better option. It allows you to build wealth gradually over time and take advantage of the power of compounding.

If you are looking to make quick profits or have a higher risk tolerance, short-term investing may be more appealing. However, it's important to remember that short-term investing can be risky and requires a significant amount of time and effort to be successful.

Long-term and short-term investing are two different approaches to investing in the stock market, and each has its own set of benefits and drawbacks. When choosing your investment strategy, it's important to consider your investment goals, risk tolerance, and personal preferences.

Whether you choose to invest for the long-term or the short-term, it's important to have a well-thought-out plan and a disciplined approach to investing.

22: STOCK MARKET INDEX FUNDS AND ETFS

Index funds and exchange-traded funds (ETFs) have become increasingly popular among investors in recent years. In this chapter, we will discuss what index funds and ETFs are and how they can be used to invest in the stock market.

INDEX FUNDS

An index fund is a type of mutual fund that tracks a specific market index, such as the S&P 500 or the Dow Jones Industrial Average.

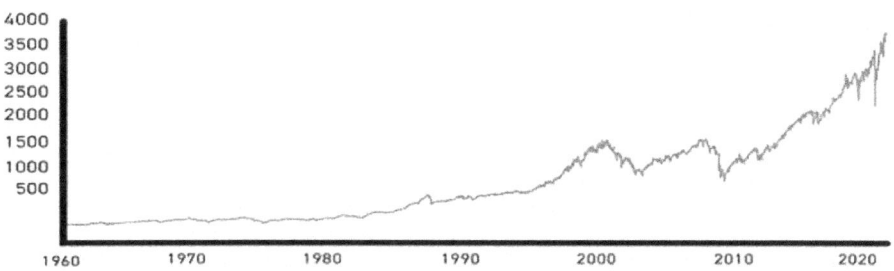

S&P Index Historical Chart. Image: centerpointsecurities.com

The goal of an index fund is to replicate the performance of the index it tracks by investing in the same stocks in the same proportion as the index.

One of the primary advantages of index funds is that they offer investors exposure to a broad range of stocks in a single investment. This diversification helps to reduce risk by spreading investments across multiple stocks, sectors, and industries.

Another advantage of index funds is their low fees. Because index funds simply track an index rather than trying to outperform it, they require less active management, resulting in lower fees and expenses.

EXCHANGE TRADED FUNDS (ETFs)

ETFs are similar to index funds in that they track a specific index, but they trade like individual stocks on an exchange.

ETFs are designed to provide investors with exposure to a specific market segment or asset class, such as large-cap stocks or emerging markets.

One of the key benefits of ETFs is their flexibility. They can be bought and sold throughout the trading day, just like individual stocks, making them a popular choice for short-term traders.

Another advantage of ETFs is their low fees. Like index funds, ETFs have lower fees than actively managed funds, making them an attractive option for cost-conscious investors.

CHOOSING THE RIGHT FUND

When choosing an index fund or ETF, there are several factors to consider. First, consider the index that the fund tracks. Make sure it aligns with your investment goals and is diversified across multiple sectors and industries.

Next, consider the fees and expenses associated with the fund. Look for funds with low expense ratios and transaction costs.

Finally, consider the track record of the fund. Look for funds with a consistent history of performance and consider the fund's risk profile and volatility.

Index funds and ETFs are popular investment vehicles that offer investors exposure to a broad range of stocks in a single investment. They are known for their low fees, diversification, and flexibility.

When choosing an index fund or ETF, it's important to consider the index it tracks, the fees and expenses associated with the fund, and the fund's performance history.

23: UNDERSTANDING FINANCIAL STATEMENTS

Financial statements are a crucial tool for investors to evaluate the financial health of a company. In this chapter, we will discuss the three main financial statements – the income statement, balance sheet, and cash flow statement – and how to interpret them.

INCOME STATEMENT

The income statement, also known as the profit and loss (P&L) statement, shows a company's revenues, expenses, and net income or loss over a specific period. It provides investors with a snapshot of a company's profitability.

The income statement includes revenues, cost of goods sold, gross profit, operating expenses, operating income, taxes, and net income. Revenues are the total amount of money a company earns from its operations, while the cost of goods sold is the direct cost of producing those goods or services.

Gross profit is the difference between revenues and cost of goods sold. Operating expenses are the indirect costs associated with running a business, such as rent, utilities, and salaries. Operating income is the company's income after deducting operating expenses.

BALANCE SHEET

The balance sheet shows a company's assets, liabilities, and equity at a specific point in time. It provides investors with a snapshot of a company's financial position.

The balance sheet includes assets, liabilities, and equity. Assets are the resources a company owns, such as cash, investments, property, and equipment. Liabilities are the company's debts, such as loans, accounts payable, and taxes owed. Equity is the residual value of a company's assets after its liabilities are paid off.

The balance sheet equation is Assets = Liabilities + Equity, which means that a company's assets must equal its liabilities plus equity at any given time.

CASH FLOW STATEMENT

The cash flow statement shows a company's cash inflows and outflows over a specific period. It provides investors with a snapshot of a company's liquidity.

The cash flow statement includes cash flow from operating activities, investing activities, and financing activities. Operating activities include the cash flows from a company's core operations, such as selling goods or services.

Investing activities include the cash flows from buying or selling assets, such as property or equipment. Financing activities include the cash flows from raising capital, such as issuing stocks or taking out loans.

INTERPRETING FINANCIAL STATEMENTS

When interpreting financial statements, investors should consider several factors, including the company's revenue growth, profitability, debt levels, and cash flow. They should also compare the company's financial performance to its competitors and the industry as a whole.

Financial statements are a crucial tool for investors to evaluate a company's financial health. The income statement shows a company's profitability, the balance sheet shows its financial position, and the cash flow statement shows its liquidity.

When interpreting financial statements, investors should consider several factors, including revenue growth, profitability, debt levels, and cash flow, and compare the company's financial performance to its competitors and the industry as a whole.

24: BASICS OF INCOME INVESTING

Income investing is an investment strategy that focuses on generating regular and stable income through the purchase of assets that pay interest, dividends, or other types of distributions. One of the most common types of income-generating assets is stocks that pay dividends.

In this chapter, we will discuss the basics of income investing in stocks, including the benefits and risks of this strategy, and some tips for investors who are interested in pursuing this investment approach.

WHAT ARE DIVIDEND-PAYING STOCKS?

Dividend-paying stocks are stocks that pay regular dividends to their shareholders. Dividends are a portion of a company's profits that are distributed to shareholders, usually on a quarterly basis. Companies that pay dividends tend to be established and stable, with a track record of consistent earnings and cash flows.

Dividend yields are calculated as a percentage of the stock price, and they can vary depending on the company's financial performance and dividend policy. Some companies pay higher dividends to attract investors, while others may reinvest their profits in the business to fuel growth.

THE BENEFITS OF INVESTING IN DIVIDEND-PAYING STOCKS

One of the primary benefits of investing in dividend-paying stocks is the regular and predictable income they provide. Dividend payments can provide a steady stream of income that can help investors meet their financial goals, such as saving for retirement or generating passive income.

Dividend-paying stocks can also provide diversification benefits to an investment portfolio. By including dividend-paying stocks in a portfolio, investors can spread their risk across different sectors and asset classes and reduce their exposure to any one stock or market.

In addition, dividend-paying stocks tend to be less volatile than growth stocks, which can experience large price swings based on changes in market sentiment and investor expectations.

By focusing on stocks that provide a stable income stream, investors can reduce the risk of losing money in the short term and achieve more predictable long-term returns.

RISKS OF INVESTING IN DIVIDEND-PAYING STOCKS

While investing in dividend-paying stocks can provide many benefits, it is not without its risks. One of the main risks of investing in dividend-paying stocks is the risk of a dividend cut or suspension. Companies can reduce or suspend their dividends for various reasons, such as declining profits, increasing debt levels, or a shift in strategic priorities. A dividend cut or suspension can lead to a decline in the stock price and a reduction in the investor's income stream.

Another risk of investing in dividend-paying stocks is the risk of market volatility. While dividend-paying stocks tend to be less volatile than growth stocks, they can still experience significant price swings based on changes in market conditions, interest rates, and investor sentiment.

Finally, investing in dividend-paying stocks can also carry stock-specific risks, such as poor management, product obsolescence, or legal and regulatory issues. It is important for investors to research individual stocks and their underlying companies before investing to understand these risks.

TIPS FOR INVESTING IN DIVIDEND-PAYING STOCKS

If you are interested in income investing in stocks, here are some tips to help you get started:

1. **Look for established and stable companies**: Companies that have a long history of paying dividends and generating consistent earnings and cash flows are often a good choice for income investors.

2. **Consider dividend growth**: Companies that have a track record of increasing their dividends over time can provide even greater income growth potential. Look for companies with a history of regular dividend increases.

3. **Evaluate the dividend yield**: The dividend yield is a measure of how much a company pays in dividends relative to its stock price. While a high dividend yield may be attractive, it is important to evaluate whether the yield is sustainable and whether the company can continue to pay dividends at that level.

4. **Diversify your portfolio**: Investing in a variety of dividend-paying stocks across different sectors and asset classes can help reduce the risk of losing money in any one stock or market.

5. **Monitor your investments:** Investing in dividend-paying stocks requires ongoing monitoring to ensure that the companies in which you have invested continue to meet your investment objectives. Here are some key factors to monitor:

6. **Earnings and cash flow:** A company's ability to generate earnings and cash flow is a key driver of its ability to pay dividends. Monitor a company's financial performance regularly to ensure that it has the capacity to maintain or increase its dividend payments.

7. **Dividend policy:** A company's dividend policy can change over time, so it's important to monitor any changes in the company's approach to dividend payments. For example, a company may decide to reduce or suspend its dividend to fund a major acquisition or expansion.

8. **Industry trends:** Economic and industry trends can affect the performance of dividend-paying stocks. Monitor industry trends and macroeconomic indicators to understand how they may impact your investment portfolio.

9. **Valuation:** Valuation is the process of assessing a company's worth. It's important to monitor the valuation of dividend-paying stocks to ensure that you are not overpaying for shares.

Income investing in stocks can provide a reliable and predictable income stream for investors. By investing in dividend-paying stocks, investors can benefit from the stability and diversification benefits of these assets, while potentially generating long-term growth.

However, it's important for investors to research individual companies and monitor their investments regularly to ensure that they continue to meet their investment objectives.

By following these basic principles, investors can build a diversified and sustainable income-generating portfolio of dividend-paying stocks.

25: PRINCIPLE OF VALUE INVESTING

Value investing is a strategy that has been used by many successful investors, including Warren Buffett and Benjamin Graham. The principle of value investing is based on the idea that a company's intrinsic value can be determined by analyzing its financial statements and other relevant information.

By identifying companies that are undervalued by the market, value investors can purchase stocks at a discount and potentially earn higher returns than the overall market.

In this chapter, we will discuss the principle of value investing, its key components, and some tips for investors looking to apply this strategy.

WHAT IS VALUE INVESTING?

Value investing is a strategy that involves buying stocks that are undervalued by the market. Value investors believe that the market is not always efficient in pricing stocks and that there are opportunities to buy stocks at a discount. They seek to identify companies that are trading at a discount to their intrinsic value and purchase those stocks with the expectation that the market will eventually recognize the company's true value, resulting in a higher stock price.

KEY COMPONENTS OF VALUE INVESTING

1. **FUNDAMENTAL ANALYSIS**

The foundation of value investing is fundamental analysis, which involves analyzing a company's financial statements, industry trends, and competitive landscape. By understanding a company's financial health, value investors can determine whether a company is undervalued by the market.

2. MARGIN OF SAFETY

One of the key concepts in value investing is the margin of safety. This refers to the difference between a company's intrinsic value and its market price. Value investors look for companies with a significant margin of safety, which provides a cushion against any potential downside risks.

3. LONG-TERM HORIZON

Value investing is a long-term strategy. Value investors are not looking to make quick profits but rather to buy and hold undervalued stocks for an extended period of time. This allows the market to recognize the company's true value and provides an opportunity for investors to earn higher returns.

TIPS FOR VALUE INVESTING

1. **Focus on Quality**: Value investors should focus on high-quality companies that have a strong competitive advantage and a history of consistent earnings. These companies are more likely to withstand economic downturns and have a higher probability of delivering long-term returns.

2. **Look for Margin of Safety**: As mentioned earlier, the margin of safety is a critical component of value investing. Investors should look for companies that are trading at a discount to their intrinsic value, providing a significant margin of safety.

3. **Avoid Herd Mentality**: Value investors should avoid following the crowd and investing in popular stocks. Instead, they should focus on companies that are undervalued by the market and have the potential for long-term growth.

4. **Be Patient**: Value investing requires patience. It can take time for the market to recognize a company's true value, and investors should be prepared to hold on to their investments for an extended period of time.

5. **Monitor Investments**: Even though value investing is a long-term strategy, investors should still monitor their investments regularly. This allows investors to make informed decisions about when to buy, hold, or sell a stock.

Value investing is a time-tested strategy that has been used by many successful investors. By focusing on fundamental analysis, margin of safety, and a long-term horizon, value investors can identify undervalued stocks and potentially earn higher returns than the overall market.

However, it is important to note that value investing is not without risks, and investors should do their due diligence and understand the potential downsides of this strategy. By following the tips outlined in this chapter, investors can make informed decisions about whether value investing is a suitable strategy for their investment goals and risk tolerance.

26: THE CONTRARIAN INVESTOR

Contrarian investing is an investment strategy that goes against the grain of popular opinion. It involves buying stocks that are out of favor with the market, often because of negative news or investor sentiment.

In this chapter, we will discuss the principles of contrarian investing and how to be a successful contrarian stock investor.

1: FOCUS ON VALUE, NOT HYPE

Contrarian investors focus on value, not hype. They look for stocks that are undervalued by the market and have a potential for long-term growth. This means they may invest in stocks that are currently out of favor with the market, but have solid fundamentals and good long-term growth prospects.

To identify undervalued stocks, contrarian investors use a variety of valuation metrics, such as price-to-earnings ratio (P/E ratio), price-to-sales ratio (P/S ratio), and price-to-book ratio (P/B ratio). These metrics help investors identify stocks that are trading at a discount to their intrinsic value.

Contrarian investors also look for companies with a strong competitive advantage and a solid management team. They believe that these factors can help a company weather short-term market volatility and position it for long-term success.

Contrarian investing requires patience and discipline, as it may take time for the market to recognize the value of an undervalued stock. Investors must be willing to hold onto their investments for the long-term, even if the stock price experiences short-term fluctuations or if the market continues to be bearish on the stock.

2: IGNORE SHORT-TERM MARKET TRENDS

In contrast to the majority of investors who follow popular trends and buy stocks that are currently in favor with the market, contrarian investors take a different approach. They ignore short-term market trends and instead focus on long-term fundamentals. They understand that the market can be driven by short-term emotions and can be irrational at times, which means that a stock can be oversold in the short-term, but still have solid long-term growth prospects.

Contrarian investors use this to their advantage by buying stocks that are currently out of favor with the market, but have strong long-term growth potential. They are willing to invest in stocks that may have fallen out of favor due to negative news or temporary setbacks, but that still have solid fundamentals and good long-term growth prospects.

One example of contrarian investing is buying stocks that are currently undervalued by the market. To identify undervalued stocks, contrarian investors use a variety of valuation metrics, such as price-to-earnings ratio (P/E ratio), price-to-sales ratio (P/S ratio), and price-to-book ratio (P/B ratio). These metrics help investors identify stocks that are trading at a discount to their intrinsic value.

3: BE SKEPTICAL OF POPULAR OPINION

Contrarian investors are skeptical of popular opinion and do their own research. They understand that the market can be influenced by media hype, analyst reports, and investor sentiment. This means that a stock can be overvalued based on popular opinion, but still have weak fundamentals.

Contrarian investors use this to their advantage by doing their own research and making their own investment decisions. They are not afraid to go against popular opinion if they believe it is based on flawed reasoning or incomplete information.

To make informed investment decisions, contrarian investors analyze a company's financial statements, management team, competitive landscape, and industry trends. They look for companies with strong balance sheets, low debt levels, and sustainable competitive advantages. They also consider macroeconomic factors, such as interest rates, inflation, and political risks, that can impact the company's future growth prospects.

4: HAVE A LONG-TERM PERSPECTIVE

Contrarian investors have a long-term perspective and are patient investors. They understand that the market can be volatile in the short-term, but that solid fundamentals and good long-term growth prospects will eventually be recognized by the market.

Contrarian investors use this to their advantage by buying undervalued stocks and holding onto them for the long-term. They have the patience to wait for the market to recognize the value of their investments, which can result in significant long-term gains.

Additionally, contrarian investors have a disciplined approach to investing. They have a clear understanding of their investment goals and risk tolerance, and they stick to their investment strategy. They avoid making impulsive decisions based on short-term market movements or emotions, which can lead to costly mistakes.

5: MANAGE RISK

Contrarian investors manage risk by diversifying their portfolio and using stop-loss orders. They understand that investing in contrarian stocks can be risky, and that not all of their investments will be successful.

Contrarian investors use this to their advantage by diversifying their portfolio across different sectors and asset classes. They also use stop-loss orders to limit their losses if a stock does not perform as expected.

A stop-loss order, as discussed in previous chapters, is an instruction to sell a stock when it reaches a certain price. It is used as a risk management tool to limit losses in case the stock price goes down. For example, if an investor buys a stock at $50 per share and sets a stop-loss order at $45 per share, the stock will automatically be sold if its price drops to $45 or below. This means that the investor's maximum loss will be limited to $5 per share.

Contrarian investors also understand the importance of monitoring their investments and adjusting their portfolio as needed. They regularly review their holdings and make changes based on changes in market conditions and company fundamentals.

Overall, contrarian investing requires a unique mindset and approach to investing. By focusing on value, doing their own research, having a long-term perspective, managing risk, and being patient, contrarian investors can potentially generate significant long-term gains. However, it is important to note that investing always carries risk, and investors should carefully consider their investment goals and risk tolerance before making any investment decisions.

6: LOOK FOR CATALYSTS

In addition to focusing on value and long-term fundamentals, contrarian investors also look for potential catalysts that can unlock value in undervalued stocks. These catalysts can come in various forms, such as a change in management, a new product launch, or a strategic acquisition.

By identifying undervalued stocks that have the potential for a positive catalyst, contrarian investors can position themselves for significant long-term gains. For example, if a company with solid fundamentals and strong growth prospects experiences a change in management, the new leadership could unlock value by implementing more efficient strategies, cutting costs, or improving operations.

Similarly, a new product launch or a strategic acquisition could also be a catalyst for a stock's growth. If a company introduces a new innovative product that captures a significant market share or acquires a competitor to gain a larger market share, the market could recognize the value of the company and the stock price could rise.

Contrarian investors have the patience to wait for the catalyst to materialize and are not afraid to take a contrarian position. They understand that the market can be inefficient and that there may be opportunities to profit from market mispricing.

By identifying undervalued stocks with potential catalysts, contrarian investors can position themselves for significant long-term gains. However, it's important to note that not all catalysts will result in positive outcomes and that investing in contrarian stocks can still be risky.

As with any investment, it's important to do thorough research and manage risk appropriately.

27: INVESTING IN IPOS

Initial Public Offerings (IPOs) are one of the most exciting events in the stock market world. They represent the first time that a company's shares are offered to the public for purchase. IPOs offer investors an opportunity to get in on the ground floor of a potentially lucrative investment opportunity. However, investing in IPOs is not without risks.

In this chapter, we will explore the pros and cons of investing in IPOs and provide some tips for those considering investing in them.

ADVANTAGES OF INVESTING IN IPOS

1. POTENTIAL FOR HIGH RETURNS

One of the primary reasons that investors are attracted to IPOs is the potential for high returns. When a company first goes public, the demand for its shares can be high, which can drive up the price.

If the company is successful in its early years, the value of its shares can increase significantly, leading to substantial returns for early investors.

2. ACCESS TO EMERGING COMPANIES

IPOs offer investors an opportunity to invest in emerging companies that have a lot of potential for growth. Many companies that go public are young and have innovative ideas that can disrupt existing industries. By investing in these companies early on, investors can potentially benefit from their success in the future.

3. DIVERSIFICATION

Investing in IPOs can provide diversification benefits to investors. As IPOs typically represent newly public companies, they can offer exposure to sectors and industries that may not be well-represented in an investor's existing portfolio.

DISADVANTAGIES OF INVESTING IN IPOS

1. LACK OF INFORMATION

One of the biggest risks of investing in IPOs is the lack of information available to investors. Unlike established companies, which have a track record of financial performance, IPOs are often untested in the public markets. As a result, it can be difficult for investors to assess the risks associated with an IPO.

2. PRICE VOLATILITY

Another significant risk associated with investing in IPOs is price volatility. As mentioned earlier, the demand for shares in a newly public company can be high, which can drive up the price. However, once the hype dies down, the price can quickly drop, leaving investors with losses.

3. LOCK-UP PERIODS

Finally, investors in IPOs may be subject to lock-up periods, during which they are not allowed to sell their shares. This can be frustrating for investors who may want to sell their shares and realize a profit but are unable to do so.

TIPS FOR INVESTING IN IPOS

1. DO YOUR DUE DILIGENCE

As with any investment, it is essential to do your due diligence before investing in an IPO. Research the company's financials, management team, and competitive landscape to assess its potential for success.

2. BE PATIENT

Investing in IPOs requires patience. It can take time for newly public companies to establish themselves and generate returns for investors. As such, it is important to have a long-term investment horizon when investing in IPOs.

3. CONSIDER THE RISKS

As discussed earlier, investing in IPOs is not without risks. Before investing, it is essential to understand the risks associated with the investment and consider whether they are acceptable given your investment goals and risk tolerance.

4. CONSIDER INVESTING IN IPO FUNDS

If you are interested in investing in IPOs but are unsure of which individual companies to invest in, you may want to consider investing in an IPO fund. These funds invest in a portfolio of newly public companies, providing diversification benefits to investors.

Investing in IPOs can be an exciting and potentially lucrative opportunity for investors. However, it is important to understand the risks associated with these investments and to do your due diligence before investing.

By considering the pros and cons of investing in IPOs and following the tips outlined in this chapter, investors can make informed decisions about whether IPOs are a suitable investment strategy for their individual financial goals and risk tolerance.

28: INVESTING WITH MUTUAL FUNDS

Investing in stocks can be a lucrative opportunity, but it can also be quite daunting. With the sheer amount of information available, it can be difficult to know where to begin. This is where mutual funds come in.

Mutual funds offer a way for investors to invest in a diversified portfolio of stocks, managed by professional fund managers.

In this chapter, we will discuss the principles of investing in stocks with mutual funds.

1: DIVERSIFICATION

Mutual funds offer diversification, which is the practice of spreading your investments across multiple asset classes and sectors. By investing in a mutual fund, you are investing in a portfolio of stocks managed by a professional fund manager.

This portfolio will typically include stocks from a variety of sectors and industries, which can help to mitigate risk.

2: PROFESSIONAL MANAGEMENT

Mutual funds are managed by professional fund managers who have the knowledge and expertise to make informed investment decisions. These managers have access to a vast array of information and resources, which can help them to identify potential investments and make sound investment decisions.

3: LOWER TRANSACTION COSTS

Mutual funds can offer lower transaction costs than investing in individual stocks. When you buy and sell individual stocks, you have to pay transaction fees, such as commissions and bid-ask spreads. These fees can add up over time and eat into your returns. With mutual funds, these fees are typically lower, as the fund manager is buying and selling stocks in bulk.

4: EASE OF INVESTING

Investing in mutual funds is easy and accessible. Most mutual funds can be bought and sold through an online brokerage account, making it easy for investors to access a diversified portfolio of stocks. Additionally, mutual funds can be purchased with small amounts of money, making it accessible to investors with limited funds.

5: DIFFERENT TYPES OF FUNDS

There are different types of mutual funds, each with its own investment objective and strategy. Some funds focus on growth, while others focus on value. Some funds invest in large-cap stocks, while others focus on small-cap stocks. By choosing the right fund, investors can tailor their investments to their investment goals and risk tolerance.

6: FEES AND EXPENSES

While mutual funds offer many benefits, it is important to consider the fees and expenses associated with investing in a mutual fund. These fees can include management fees, administrative expenses, and other charges. It is important to understand these fees and expenses before investing in a mutual fund.

7: PERFORMANCE

When considering investing in a mutual fund, it is important to consider its historical performance. This can give investors an idea of how the fund has performed in the past and what its potential for future returns may be. It is important to remember that past performance is not a guarantee of future results, but it can give investors an idea of what to expect.

Investing in stocks with mutual funds can be a great way for investors to gain exposure to the stock market without having to research individual stocks or manage a portfolio on their own.

By offering diversification, professional management, lower transaction costs, ease of investing, different types of funds, fees and expenses, and performance, mutual funds can be a valuable investment tool for investors of all levels.

As with any investment, it is important to do your research and understand the risks and potential rewards before investing in a mutual fund.

29: MARGIN TRADING

Margin trading is a type of stock investing that involves borrowing money from a broker to buy stocks. With margin trading, you can potentially increase your investment returns by using leverage, but it also comes with increased risk. Here are some key things to know about margin trading:

HOW MARGIN TRADING WORKS

When you open a margin account with a broker, you're able to borrow money to buy stocks.

The securities themselves serve as collateral for the loan. The amount of money you can borrow is determined by the broker's margin requirements, which typically specify a minimum percentage of the total value of the securities being purchased that must be put down as collateral.

For example, if the broker's margin requirement is 50%, and you want to purchase $10,000 worth of stock, you would need to put down $5,000 in cash as collateral and borrow the remaining $5,000 from the broker.

This means that you would have a leverage ratio of 2:1, as your total investment would be worth $15,000 ($10,000 in stock plus $5,000 borrowed from the broker).

The main appeal of margin trading is that it allows investors to amplify their returns by using borrowed funds to increase their exposure to the market.

For example, let's say you have $10,000 in cash to invest and you use it to purchase $10,000 worth of stock. If the stock rises 10%, you have made a $1,000 profit.

However, if you had used margin to purchase $20,000 worth of stock with the same $10,000, and the stock rises by 10%, you would have made a $2,000 profit - twice as much as you would have without margin.

MARGIN TRADING RISKS

However, this strategy also carries significant risks. If the stock price were to fall instead of rise, you could suffer much larger losses than you would have without margin.

This is because the broker will typically issue a margin call if the value of the securities being held as collateral falls below a certain threshold. If this happens, the investor will be required to deposit additional funds to bring the collateral back up to the required level.

If the investor cannot meet this margin call, the broker may sell off the securities to cover the loan, which could result in significant losses.

Another risk of margin trading is that it can magnify the impact of volatility on an investor's portfolio. If the market experiences a sharp downturn, highly leveraged investors may find themselves facing substantial losses, potentially wiping out their entire investment capital and even incurring a debt to the broker.

It is important to note that margin trading is not suitable for all investors. It is a high-risk strategy that requires a lot of knowledge, experience, and discipline.

It is only recommended for experienced traders who have a good understanding of market trends and can afford to lose the money they invest.

MARGIN TRADING TIPS

If you're considering margin trading, here are some tips to keep in mind:

Only invest what you can afford to lose

Margin trading is a high-risk strategy, so it's important to only invest money that you can afford to lose.

Understand your broker's margin requirements

Different brokers have different margin requirements, so make sure you understand how much you can borrow and what the margin call requirements are.

Diversify your portfolio

Diversifying your portfolio can help reduce risk, even when using margin trading. Consider investing in a mix of stocks, bonds, and other assets to spread out your risk.

Have a plan for managing risk

Before you start margin trading, have a plan in place for managing risk. This may include setting stop-loss orders to limit losses or having a plan for how much you're willing to lose before selling your holdings.

Margin trading can potentially increase investment returns, but it also comes with increased risk. Before considering margin trading, it's important to understand the risks involved and have a plan in place for managing risk.

Only invest what you can afford to lose and make sure you're comfortable with your broker's margin requirements before getting started.

With roper preparation and a conservative approach, margin trading can be a valuable tool for investors looking to maximize their returns.

30: YOUR EXIT STRATEGY

While many investors focus heavily on choosing the right stocks to buy, it is just as important to have a plan in place for selling them when the time is right. In this chapter, we will explore what an exit strategy is, why it is important, and how to develop a strategy that works for you.

WHAT IS AN EXIT STRATEGY?

An exit strategy is a plan for selling your stock investments at the right time. This can involve selling all of your shares, or just a portion of them, depending on your goals and circumstances. An exit strategy should be based on a number of factors, including your investment objectives, risk tolerance, and the current state of the market.

WHY IS AN EXIT STRATEGY IMPORTANT?

There are a number of reasons why having an exit strategy is important. Perhaps the most important reason is that it can help you avoid emotional decision-making. When the market is volatile and stock prices are fluctuating, it can be tempting to sell your investments in a panic or hold onto them for too long in the hopes that they will recover. Having a pre-determined plan in place can help you avoid making impulsive decisions that could negatively impact your portfolio.

An exit strategy can also help you take profits at the right time. While it is important to let your investments grow over time, it is equally important to lock in profits when the market is performing well.

By selling your shares at the right time, you can ensure that you are not holding onto investments that have already peaked, and can instead use those profits to invest in new opportunities or diversify your portfolio.

Finally, having an exit strategy can help you limit your losses. If you have a plan in place for selling your shares if they fall below a certain price, you can protect yourself from significant losses if the market experiences a downturn.

HOW TO DEVELOP AN EXIT STRATEGY

Developing an exit strategy requires careful planning and consideration. Here are some steps you can take to create a strategy that works for you:

1. **DETERMINE YOUR INVESTMENT GOALS**

    Before you can develop an exit strategy, you need to know what your investment goals are. Are you investing for short-term gains or long-term growth? Are you focused on income or capital appreciation? Your goals will influence the types of stocks you invest in, and when you choose to sell them.

2. **SET YOUR RISK TOLERANCE**

    Your risk tolerance is the amount of risk you are willing to take on in pursuit of your investment goals. This will also influence when and how you choose to sell your investments.

3. **IDENTIFY YOUR CRITERIA FOR SELLING**

    Once you have established your investment goals and risk tolerance, you need to identify the criteria that will trigger a sell. This might include hitting a certain price target, experiencing a certain level of volatility, or seeing a negative trend in the company's financials.

4. **DETERMINE YOUR SELLING STRATEGY**

There are a number of strategies you can use to sell your stocks, including selling all of your shares at once, selling a portion of your shares incrementally, or using stop-loss orders to sell your shares automatically if they fall below a certain price.

5. MONITOR AND ADJUST YOUR STRATEGY

Your exit strategy should not be set in stone. As market conditions change and your investment goals evolve, you may need to adjust your strategy to stay on track.

Having an exit strategy is a critical component of any successful stock investment strategy. By developing a plan for when and how to sell your shares, you can avoid emotional decision-making, take profits at the right time, and limit your losses.

When developing your exit strategy, it is important to consider your investment goals, risk tolerance, and criteria for selling, and to remain flexible as market conditions change over time.

31: ONLINE STOCK TRADING

Online stock trading has become a popular way for individuals to invest in the stock market. Thanks to advancements in technology, it's now possible to buy and sell stocks from anywhere in the world, using only an internet connection and a computer or smartphone.

In this chapter, we'll explore the benefits and risks of online stock trading, as well as some tips for getting started.

Image: pexel.com

BENEFITS OF ONLINE STOCK TRADING

One of the main benefits of online stock trading is the convenience it offers. With an online brokerage account, traders can access real-time market data, research stocks, and execute trades from anywhere in the world. This means that traders no longer need to be physically present at a brokerage firm to buy and sell stocks, which can save time and money.

Another benefit of online stock trading is the low fees and commissions offered by many online brokers. Traditional brokerage firms often charge high fees for each trade, which can eat into profits. Online brokers, on the other hand, often offer lower fees and commissions, which can save traders money in the long run.

Online trading platforms also offer a range of tools and resources to help traders make informed decisions. Many platforms provide real-time news and market analysis, as well as research reports and trading ideas. Some even offer educational resources and courses to help beginners learn the basics of trading.

RISKS OF ONLINE STOCK TRADING

While online stock trading offers many benefits, it's important to be aware of the risks involved.

One of the main risks is emotional trading. Online traders may be more prone to making impulsive decisions, as the ease of access and immediacy of trades can lead to emotional trading. This can result in buying or selling stocks based on fear or greed, rather than sound analysis and research.

Another risk of online stock trading is technical issues. Connectivity problems or software glitches can cause trades to be executed improperly or not at all. This can result in losses for traders who are unable to buy or sell stocks at the desired price.

It's important for online traders to have a solid trading plan in place and to be aware of technical issues that may arise.

TIPS FOR GETTING STARTED WITH ONLINE STOCK TRADING

If you're interested in online stock trading, there are a few things you can do to get started. Here are some tips:

Do your research

Before getting started, it's important to do your research and learn as much as you can about trading. This can involve reading books, attending courses, and studying market analysis and news.

Choose a reputable online broker

There are many online brokers to choose from, so it's important to choose a reputable one that offers low fees and commissions, as well as a user-friendly platform.

Set a trading plan

Before making any trades, it's important to set a trading plan that outlines your goals, risk tolerance, and strategy. This can help prevent emotional trading and ensure that you stay on track.

Practice with a demo account

Many online brokers offer demo accounts that allow you to practice trading without risking real money. This can be a great way to get a feel for the platform and test out your trading strategy before investing real money.

Start small

When you're ready to start trading with real money, it's important to start small and only invest money that you can afford to lose. This can help minimize risk and prevent you from making impulsive decisions.

Online stock trading can be a convenient and cost-effective way to invest in the stock market. However, it's important to be aware of the risks involved and to have a solid trading plan in place.

By doing your research, choosing a reputable online broker, setting a trading plan, and starting small, you can increase your chances of success in online stock trading.

32: THE ROLE OF NEWS AND MEDIA IN THE STOCK MARKET

News and media play a significant role in the stock market. Investors rely on news and media to make informed decisions about buying and selling stocks. In this chapter, we will discuss the impact of news and media on the stock market and how to evaluate the credibility of news sources.

IMPACT OF NEWS & MEDIA ON THE STOCK MARKET

News and media can have a significant impact on the stock market. Positive news, such as a company's strong earnings report or a successful product launch, can lead to an increase in stock prices. Negative news, such as a company's bankruptcy filing or a global economic downturn, can lead to a decrease in stock prices.

The speed at which news spreads in the age of social media and instant communication can also impact the stock market. A tweet or news article can cause a sudden surge or decline in a stock's price. This is known as a "flash crash," and it highlights the importance of staying informed and making quick decisions in the stock market.

EVALUATING THE CREDIBILITY OF NEWS SOURCES

Not all news sources are credible, and it's essential to evaluate the reliability of the news before making any investment decisions. Here are some tips for evaluating the credibility of news sources:

Look for unbiased sources

Look for sources that are unbiased and not affiliated with any particular company or interest group.

Check the author's credentials

Check the author's credentials and reputation to ensure they are credible and have expertise in the topic they are discussing.

Consider the source's reputation

Consider the reputation of the news source itself. Is it known for producing reliable and accurate reporting, or does it have a history of sensationalism or bias?

Check multiple sources

Check multiple sources to ensure the accuracy of the information being presented.

Watch for clickbait headlines

Be wary of clickbait headlines that are designed to grab your attention but may not accurately represent the content of the article.

News and media play a crucial role in the stock market, and investors rely on them to make informed decisions. Positive and negative news can impact stock prices, and the speed at which news spreads can cause sudden surges or declines in stock prices. It's important to evaluate the credibility of news sources before making any investment decisions.

Looking for unbiased sources, checking the author's credentials, considering the source's reputation, checking multiple sources, and watching for clickbait headlines are all essential steps to ensure the accuracy of the information being presented.

33: TAX IMPLICATIONS OF STOCK MARKET INVESTING

Investing in the stock market can be a great way to grow your wealth, but it's important to be aware of the tax implications of your investments. In this chapter, we will discuss the various taxes that apply to stock market investments and strategies for minimizing your tax liability.

CAPITAL GAINS TAX

When you sell a stock at a profit, you will be subject to capital gains tax. The capital gains tax rate depends on how long you hold the stock before selling it. If you hold the stock for more than one year, you will be subject to long-term capital gains tax rates, which are generally lower than short-term capital gains tax rates.

DIVIDEND TAX

If you receive dividends from your stock investments, you will be subject to dividend tax. The dividend tax rate depends on your income level and the type of dividend you receive. Qualified dividends are taxed at long-term capital gains tax rates, while non-qualified dividends are taxed at ordinary income tax rates.

STRATEGIES FOR MINIMIZING TAX LIABILITY

There are several strategies for minimizing your tax liability when investing in the stock market:

Use tax-advantaged accounts

Consider investing in tax-advantaged accounts such as individual retirement accounts (IRAs) or 401(k) plans. These accounts offer tax benefits that can help reduce your overall tax liability.

Hold stocks for more than one year

If possible, hold your stocks for more than one year to take advantage of long-term capital gains tax rates.

Reinvest dividends

Instead of taking dividends as cash, consider reinvesting them into the same stock or another investment. This can help defer taxes on your dividends.

Tax-loss harvesting

If you have investments that have lost value, consider selling them to offset capital gains taxes on profitable investments.

Seek professional advice

Consider seeking the advice of a tax professional to help you develop a tax-efficient investment strategy.

Investing in the stock market can have significant tax implications, and it's important to be aware of the taxes that apply to your investments. Capital gains tax and dividend tax are two common taxes that apply to stock market investments.

There are several strategies for minimizing your tax liability, including using tax-advantaged accounts, holding stocks for more than one year, reinvesting dividends, tax-loss harvesting, and seeking professional advice.

By being proactive and strategic with your investments, you can minimize your tax liability and maximize your returns.

34: THE PSYCHOLOGY OF TRADING THE STOCK MARKET

Investing in the stock market requires more than just financial knowledge and analysis. It also requires a strong understanding of human psychology. In this chapter, we will explore the psychological factors that can impact your stock market trading and offer strategies for managing these factors.

EMOTIONAL INVESTING

One of the biggest psychological challenges of stock market trading is managing your emotions. Fear, greed, and anxiety can all lead to impulsive decisions and irrational behavior, which can negatively impact your investment performance.

To manage your emotions, it's important to develop a disciplined approach to investing. This includes setting clear investment goals, developing a trading plan, and sticking to your plan even when the market is volatile. It's also important to avoid impulsive decisions, such as panic selling during a market downturn.

CONFIRMATION BIAS

Another psychological challenge of stock market trading is confirmation bias. This is the tendency to seek out information that confirms our existing beliefs and ignore information that contradicts them. Confirmation bias can lead to poor investment decisions, as it can cause investors to overlook important data and make decisions based on flawed assumptions.

To overcome confirmation bias, it's important to approach investment analysis with an open mind. Seek out diverse sources of information, consider alternative viewpoints, and be willing to revise your beliefs in light of new evidence.

LOSS AVERSION

Loss aversion is the tendency to place greater value on avoiding losses than on achieving gains. This can lead to risk aversion and a reluctance to take chances, which can negatively impact your investment performance.

To manage loss aversion, it's important to focus on your overall investment strategy rather than short-term losses. Remember that losses are a natural part of investing and that they can often be recouped over the long term.

Investing in the stock market requires a strong understanding of human psychology. Emotional investing, confirmation bias, and loss aversion are three common psychological challenges that can impact investment performance.

To overcome these challenges, it's important to develop a disciplined approach to investing, seek out diverse sources of information, and focus on your overall investment strategy rather than short-term losses.

By managing these psychological factors, you can become a more successful stock market trader.

35: COMMON MISTAKES TO AVOID

Investing in the stock market can be a rewarding experience, but it can also be fraught with risks and challenges. In this chapter, we will explore some of the common mistakes that investors make and offer strategies for avoiding them.

1. LACK OF RESEARCH

One of the biggest mistakes that investors make is not doing enough research before making investment decisions.

Failing to research a company or a stock thoroughly can lead to poor investment decisions, which can negatively impact your portfolio.

To avoid this mistake, it's important to take the time to research a company thoroughly before investing. This includes analyzing the company's financial statements, understanding its business model, and keeping up to date with industry trends.

2. EMOTIONAL INVESTING

Another common mistake that investors make is letting their emotions guide their investment decisions. Fear, greed, and anxiety can all lead to impulsive decisions and irrational behavior, which can negatively impact your investment performance.

To avoid emotional investing, it's important to develop a disciplined approach to investing. This includes setting clear investment goals, developing a trading plan, and sticking to your plan even when the market is volatile. It's also important to avoid impulsive decisions, such as panic selling during a market downturn.

3. OVERCONFIDENCE

Overconfidence is another common mistake that investors make. This is the tendency to overestimate your abilities and underestimate the risks involved in investing. Overconfidence can lead to poor investment decisions, which can negatively impact your portfolio.

To avoid overconfidence, it's important to approach investing with a humble attitude. Recognize that investing involves risks and uncertainties and that no one can predict the market with 100% accuracy. It's also important to seek out diverse sources of information and consider alternative viewpoints.

4. CHASING HOT STOCKS

Another common mistake that investors make is chasing hot stocks. This is the tendency to invest in stocks that have already experienced significant price increases in the hope that they will continue to rise.

To avoid this mistake, it's important to focus on the fundamentals of a company rather than its recent performance. This includes analyzing its financial statements, understanding its business model, and assessing its long-term growth prospects.

5. LISTENING TO NON EXPERTS

Whenever the stock market goes through an extended period of growth, there is a surge of self-proclaimed investment experts offering advice. It's important to exercise caution when seeking guidance and be selective about the source of advice you choose.

Remember, opinions are not facts, and it's crucial to distinguish between the two with a clear and unbiased mind. Even professionals can make mistakes, so the ultimate responsibility falls on you to conduct thorough research and exercise due diligence before making any investment decisions.

6. FAILING TO DIVERSIFY

Finally, failing to diversify is another common mistake that investors make. This is the tendency to invest all of your money in a single stock or a single sector, which can lead to significant losses if that stock or sector performs poorly.

To avoid this mistake, it's important to diversify your portfolio across different asset classes and sectors. This can help to reduce your overall risk and protect your portfolio from significant losses.

Investing in the stock market involves risks and challenges, but it can also be a rewarding experience. By avoiding common mistakes such as lack of research, emotional investing, overconfidence, chasing hot stocks, and failing to diversify, you can become a more successful investor and achieve your financial goals.

Remember to approach investing with a disciplined, humble attitude, and to always focus on the fundamentals of a company before making investment decisions.

36: STRATEGIES FOR SUCCESS IN STOCK MARKET INVESTING

Successful stock market investing requires patience, discipline, and a well-informed approach. While there is no foolproof formula for success, there are some strategies that can increase your chances of achieving your investment goals.

1. DO YOUR RESEARCH

Research is key to making informed investment decisions. Before investing in a company, do your due diligence by reviewing its financial statements, news articles, and market trends. Learn about the industry and its competitors. Understanding the company and its market is the first step to making informed investment decisions.

2. DIVERSIFY YOUR PORTFOLIO

A diversified portfolio spreads risk across different companies, sectors, and asset classes. It helps reduce the impact of market volatility on your investment. When one sector or asset class is underperforming, other parts of your portfolio can balance the losses. Diversification can also provide higher returns over time.

3. INVEST FOR THE LONG TERM

Investing in the stock market is a long-term game. Avoid the temptation to make quick profits by day trading or trying to time the market. Instead, focus on investing in quality companies with strong fundamentals and growth potential. Invest regularly and consistently, and let your money grow over time.

4. STICK TO YOUR PLAN

Once you have a plan in place, stick to it. Avoid making impulsive decisions based on market fluctuations or emotions. Instead, stay disciplined and keep your investment strategy on track.

5. MONITOR YOUR PORTFOLIO

Monitoring your portfolio regularly is important to ensure that your investments are performing as expected. Keep track of market trends and news that may impact your investments. Periodically review your investment strategy and make adjustments as needed.

6. PRACTICE PATIENCE

Stock market investing is not a get-rich-quick scheme. It requires patience, discipline, and a long-term perspective.

Avoid the temptation to make impulsive decisions based on short-term market trends. Instead, stay focused on your long-term investment goals.

7. LEARN FROM YOUR MISTAKES

Investing in the stock market involves some trial and error. Mistakes are part of the learning process. Use your mistakes as an opportunity to learn and improve your investment strategy.

Successful stock market investing requires discipline, patience, and a well-informed approach. Do your research, diversify your portfolio, invest for the long term, stick to your plan, monitor your portfolio, practice patience, and learn from your mistakes.

By following these strategies, you can increase your chances of achieving your investment goals over time.

37: BUILDING A STOCK PORTFOLIO

Building a stock portfolio is a crucial aspect of stock market investing. A well-diversified portfolio can help manage risk and potentially increase returns over the long term. Here are some key steps to building a successful stock portfolio:

1. **DETERMINE YOUR INVESTMENT GOALS**

Before building a stock portfolio, it's important to determine your investment goals. Are you investing for retirement or a specific financial goal, such as buying a house or funding a child's education? Your investment goals will help guide your investment decisions.

2. **DEFINE YOUR RISK TOLERANCE**

Your risk tolerance is the amount of risk you are willing to take on to achieve your investment goals. Some investors are more risk-averse and prefer to invest in lower-risk securities, while others are willing to take on more risk for the potential for higher returns. Defining your risk tolerance will help you determine the appropriate mix of securities for your portfolio.

3. **CHOOSE YOUR ASSET ALLOCATION**

Asset allocation is the process of dividing your portfolio among different asset classes, such as stocks, bonds, and cash. The allocation will depend on your investment goals, risk tolerance, and time horizon. Generally, a younger investor with a longer time horizon may be more heavily invested in stocks, while an older investor may have a greater allocation to bonds.

4. SELECT YOUR STOCKS

Once you have determined your asset allocation, you can begin selecting individual stocks. It's important to research each stock thoroughly and evaluate its financial health, growth potential, and valuation. Consider investing in a mix of large-cap, mid-cap, and small-cap stocks across different sectors and industries to diversify your portfolio.

5. MONITOR YOUR PORTFOLIO

Regularly monitoring your portfolio is critical to ensuring that it is performing as expected. Keep track of market trends and news that may impact your investments. Periodically review your investment strategy and make adjustments as needed.

6. REBALANCE YOUR PORTFOLIO

Over time, your asset allocation may shift as some investments perform better than others. Rebalancing your portfolio involves adjusting your asset allocation to bring it back in line with your investment goals and risk tolerance. This can help manage risk and potentially increase returns over the long term.

7. CONSIDER PROFESSIONAL ADVICE

If you're unsure about how to build a stock portfolio, consider consulting with a financial advisor or investment professional. They can help you determine your investment goals, risk tolerance, and asset allocation, and recommend stocks that align with your objectives.

Building a stock portfolio is an important part of stock market investing. Determine your investment goals and risk tolerance, choose your asset allocation, select your stocks, monitor and rebalance your portfolio, and consider seeking professional advice.

By following these steps, you can build a well-diversified portfolio that aligns with your investment goals and risk tolerance.

38: CONCLUSION AND NEXT STEPS

Congratulations on finishing this beginner's guide to stock market investing! You should now have a good understanding of the basics of the stock market, different types of stocks, how to read stock charts, evaluate companies and stocks, risk management strategies, developing a stock investing plan, online and offline stock trading, and many other essential topics.

However, this is just the beginning of your journey as a stock market investor. There is always more to learn and explore in the ever-changing world of finance. Here are some next steps you can take to continue your education and improve your investing skills:

Continue Your Education

Keep reading books, articles, and blogs about stock market investing. Attend webinars and seminars and take online courses to continue learning new strategies and techniques.

The more you read, the deeper you grasp the concepts and the clearer your next steps.

Start Small

Don't jump into the stock market with all your money. Start small by investing a small amount of money and see how it performs. You can gradually increase your investment as you gain more confidence and experience.

Don't try to do everything at once, pick a particular aspect that resonates with you the most and start with that.

Diversify Your Portfolio

Don't put all your eggs in one basket. Diversify your portfolio by investing in different sectors and industries. This will help you manage risk and improve your chances of making a profit.

Keep A Long-Term Perspective

Stock market investing is a long-term game. Don't get discouraged by short-term fluctuations in the market. Keep a long-term perspective and invest in companies that have a solid track record of growth.

Seek Advice From Professionals

If you're unsure about how to proceed with your investments, seek advice from a financial advisor or a stockbroker. They can help you make informed decisions and develop a strategy that fits your financial goals.

Remember, stock market investing requires patience, discipline, and a willingness to learn. It can be a rewarding experience if you take the time to educate yourself, develop a plan, and stay committed to your goals.

I wish you God's abundant blessings and peace on your journey as a stock market investor!

ABOUT THE AUTHOR

Usiere Uko

Usiere Uko is a Consultant, ILO Certified Trainer, and Business & Finance Author focused on financial independence and entrepreneurship. A former oil and gas engineer turned entrepreneur, he helps individuals and business owners build sustainable income, make smarter financial decisions, and grow resilient businesses.

He is a certified Business Development Service Provider (BDSP) and an ILO-certified trainer in SIYB and WIDB, and currently serves as Lead Consultant at Sageway Consulting and Training Coordinator at The Citadel Business Academy.

Usiere writes in a friendly and practical style, making complex financial and business ideas simple, clear, and actionable for everyday readers and entrepreneurs. He is based in Lagos, Nigeria.

BOOKS IN THIS SERIES
STOCK MARKET & REAL ASSETS

Stock Market Investing 101: A Beginner's Guide To Building Wealth With Smart Stock Investing

Real Estate Investing 101: A Simple Guide To Building Wealth With Property

BOOKS BY THIS AUTHOR

Practical Steps To Financial Freedom & Independence

A Simple Guide To Investing In The Money Market

Before You Trade Forex

Before You Invest In Cryptocurrency

101 Common Money Mistakes To Avoid

How To Invest In Bonds

How To Invest In Treasury Bills (Bonds)

How To Avoid Living Under Financial Pressure

Financial Independence For Employees

Managing Your Money Post Covid

Retire On Your Own Terms

Your Ultimate Money Makeover

Teaching Kids Money 101

Uncle Ben's Money Lessons

Nft Investing 101: A Beginner's Guide To Collectible Digital Assets

www.ingramcontent.com/pod-product-compliance
Lightning Source LLC
Chambersburg PA
CBHW050011230526
45465CB00003BB/1360